The Angels' Share

Written by Paul Laverty
Directed by Ken Loach

First published in 2012 by Route
PO Box 167, Pontefract, WF8 4WW
info@route-online.com
www.route-online.com

In association with Sixteen Films
2nd Floor, 187 Wardour Street, London, W1F 8ZB

© Screenplay: Paul Laverty

ISBN: 978-1-901927-55-9

© Photographs: Joss Barratt

Cover design:
GOLDEN www.wearegolden.co.uk
From artwork supplied by Entertainment One UK Ltd

Printed and bound by CPI Group (UK) Ltd, Croydon, CR0 4YY

Contents

Paul Laverty
Writer

Our previous film was a tragic story. With this one we wanted to explore not just another tone, but somehow to try and inhabit another register. From its first simmerings it had the feel of a little fable; at least in the imagination, it was an attempt to be realistic but also a little magical, perhaps a fable of wasted talent and what happens when we are given a chance in life. Although the characters somehow feel familiar to us, I hope there is a sense of their life force and mischief that might make you care for them.

Two central and simple situations came to mind which we thought were worth exploring. When anyone has their first child, it is a stunning experience that changes their life forever. It automatically projects into the future, and raises both practical and existential questions of the most profound nature. Past, present and future somehow become different when you have another human being to care for. The second notion: we now live in a world where many young people in particular will not have a proper job in their lives. These two situations merge in the character of Robbie and offer tremendous dramatic potential.

Robbie has had a tragic past and after a chaotic childhood we imagined he had served time in Polmont Young Offenders Institution. Is he going to repeat with his own son what he'd lived with his father and his grandfather? Third generation unemployment is not unusual in many of our cities. He's really up against it as the father of his girlfriend considers him to be a 'scumbag'. It's a big step to look at yourself and say, 'Right, am I a loser or can I make something of my life, despite what I've lived through?' There's dramatic tension there, both with the world outside, but also inside his head. Not only does the world distrust him, and for good reason, but he is not sure if he has the strength to change himself – never mind what is around him.

He needs a break. That's where the character Harry appeared. He is somebody who has lived through tough circumstances himself, having lost his business and his family. I think we can forget how much an arbitrary piece of luck – of meeting the right person at the right time – can change a life, especially if it is at a vulnerable moment. A little perception, experience and generosity of spirit can go a long way. You see it again and again: even in the preparation for this film I met older people working with youngsters who had a zest about them. Young people get it very hard in this country: they're too easily stereotyped as lazy, greedy, feckless. Harry's the type of man who sees the potential in people. Even as I was going round talking to many of the supervisors who were dealing with those doing Community Service Orders, I saw those traits. Some of the supervisors, not an easy job, were authoritarian – and got nowhere with them. But then you saw others that were creative, thought laterally, who encouraged and made them laugh. It worked much better, for some. That brought the best out of people, especially for those whom you might guess had been more shouted at in their lives than ever listened to.

Kenny MacAskill, an old friend with whom I did my legal apprenticeships nearly 30 years ago, suggested I meet a senior police officer who was running the Violence Reduction Unit in Strathclyde, a man called John Carnochan. John had great experience and had many fascinating insights that were far from the stereotype. As part of their work with gangs in Glasgow they'd looked at flashpoints and the most dangerous moments of the week, especially Friday night, when far too often cheap alcohol, adrenalin and not much to do combine in the worst manner.

So John and his colleagues ended up collaborating with people who ran football matches on a Friday night throughout the city. Better to be playing each other than fighting each other. I asked John to put me in contact with anybody who was working on that scheme and one of the many fascinating characters I met was Paul Brannigan.

He was a very bright lad, thoughtful. He'd lived through many tough experiences himself, but there was a steadiness to him. He got a bunch of the lads together from the group he was running, and it was their chance to take the piss with a filmmaker. We chatted for about two hours. It was chaotic, funny; Paul managed the boys very well. He just had a natural understated presence, and you could sense he was held with respect.

So I met him several times more, made a mental note and mentioned him to Ken. When we came to do the casting I was really keen that Paul should come along, but as it turned out that proved slightly more complicated than we imagined and no doubt he might tell the tale in his own words.

When he finally came along and did the first improvisation you could sense he had something special and as we did more and more you could see his confidence grow. He had natural charisma, a great face, and a sense of lived experience underneath: a sense of vulnerability, which was really important for the character. I will always respect how Ken is prepared to take a gamble and cast someone with no acting experience at the heart of a film. He did it with *Kes,* with *Sweet Sixteen* and now again. It takes nerve but I think Paul did us proud. There is almost a fable-like quality to how Paul got the part of Robbie too.

The whisky world is full of intriguing contradictions, which is always attractive. Ever since I heard of a flock of geese guarding a whisky warehouse it has struck me there must be some comic potential in there. I blame my brother-in-law Angus McConnel for introducing me to the wonderful world of malts, from Bladnoch in the South to Old Pulteney in the North, and many hangovers in between. At one level it is scientific, empirical and great craftsmanship. But at another there is almost a magical quality; from the specific shape of the still, to the particular barrel once steeped perhaps in Spanish sherry in a particular spot in a dunnage warehouse producing a unique whisky. There is something exotic about those thousands of barrels maturing for years in the dark, intermittently tested by the warehouse man like some magician of old. (Not the best place to spend hours shooting, ask the crew.) And those stunning distilleries by mountains, streams or facing the wild Atlantic.

The Angels' Share is a delightful notion: that precious per cent that drifts off by itself to escape Homo sapiens and the tax man. The poetic and the bullshit rub up against one another, the mythical, the marketing, the professionalism, the phoney, the snobbery, and of course the sheer genuine pleasure of it all, make for a wonderful concoction with many levels. I remember the first time I heard an old man in a scruffy pub call for 'a wee low flyer', a nip of Grouse, dwarfed by his half pint, and the smile on his face. At the other extreme a principal dealer in London told me of the Arab Prince who bought a bottle of whisky for £32,000 in an hotel in Kent and polished it off with his friends, followed by two more bottles exceeding twenty grand.

Charlie MacLean, a genuine whisky expert, and the most generous of enthusiasts, introduced me to the complexity of our own senses, and what a wonderful organ the humble nose is. Likewise the palate. Nosing and tasting whisky will never be the same. And yet despite whisky's multimillion pound international projection, and its association with our cultural identity, it amazed me how many young Scots had never tasted our national drink. But more surprising than that, many of the young people I met serving court orders had never enjoyed the countryside, mountains and glorious spots where whisky is made. Strange, both whisky and beauty, on our doorstep, but out of reach.

There are thousands of Robbies and Rhinos out there, and I like the idea they can learn to enjoy the fine things in life more than an Arab Prince, given the chance.

The Angels' Share

Screenplay

AGAINST BLACK: Sounds of solemn VOICES from inside the Sheriff Court, Glasgow.

SHERIFF CLERK

Call Albert Ridley.

COURT OFFICER

[Loud shout] Albert Ridley!

Sounds of footsteps.

SHERIFF CLERK

Are you Albert Ridley?

There is a hesitation and then a huge sneeze.

VOICE

Yes…

FISCAL

This is a slightly unusual case My Lord… the accused was at an unmanned train station under the influence of a strong fortified wine…

SHERIFF

Buckfast again?

FISCAL

Seems so My Lord… railway personnel manning security cameras from some twenty miles away saw him staggering very close to

15

the edge of the platform and realising that an
express train was to pass within minutes, tried
to warn him to stay back by the use of the
platform speakers...

1. FLASHBACK TO THE STATION: DAY

ALBERT (a dopey lad but with friendly gait that would raise a
smile, mid to late twenties) well and truly inebriated, wanders along
the edge of the platform. He balances on the very edge, wobbles
back and forth, and holds his hands out as if about to set off flying.

> VOICE FROM SPEAKERS
> Will all passengers stand back from the edge of
> the platform!

Albert looks around at the abandoned station and is totally
confused. (He doesn't see the camera mounted on a pole.)

> VOICE FROM SPEAKERS (CONT'D)
> Aye you!... Stand back... there is a train
> coming through any minute... stand back
> immediately!

Albert is even more confused and spins around in the other
direction. He seems to have taken insult at the instructions. He
gives the fingers in all directions to unseen ghosts.

> ALBERT
> Fuck you! Where are yis? Come on!

He moves even closer to the edge. Now he jumps down from the
platform and stands in the middle of track.

> VOICE FROM SPEAKERS
> This is the station master! Get off the tracks
> immediately! Get off the track! An express train
> is coming!

Albert starts doing a piss unaware of the danger. (From the back we see him swish and piss from side to side like a child.) Noise of a train in the distance.

> VOICE FROM SPEAKERS (CONT'D)
> You... with tracksuit and trainers... yes you... looking right, now left... yes you, pishing your pants you fucking imbecile!

He looks above him for an invisible voice.

> VOICE FROM SPEAKERS (CONT'D)
> [Booming, another deeper more powerful voice] This is God calling! Watching you from above... this is a message from God you bloody moron... there is an express train coming through any second... this is God ordering you to pull up your zip, climb back on to the platform now or you will never piss again!

Albert scrambles up onto the platform and manages to pull himself up. Seconds later an express train thunders through.

> ALBERT
> Fucking hell... [looking up to heavens]...yi saved ma life!

> VOICE FROM SPEAKERS
> You fucking numptie!... Get down on your knees... Down I said! Down! [Albert gets to his knees.] Beg forgiveness, and don't move till I say so!

He looks up to the sky and then blesses himself.

2. GLASGOW SHERIFF COURT – COURT 4

An acerbic and long-suffering SHERIFF with a reputation for mild eccentricity, dressed in wig and gown, sits on the raised bench.

He deals with the sentencing of a miscellaneous selection of cases. From the ordinary to slightly surreal. (Social security fraud, theft, shoplifting, traffic offences, assault and resisting arrest etc.)

Immediately below him is the SHERIFF CLERK who runs the show. The clerk calls out the names of those awaiting sentencing who make their way to the dock. There they join a burly court officer who makes sure that each of them stands to attention and responds to the namecheck when appropriate. If the case is more serious, the accused, in custody and awaiting sentencing, will appear from a different door with a guard and handcuffed to the same.

In front of the Sheriff Clerk, at a large square table is the PROCURATOR FISCAL (prosecution) on one side, and on the other, various lawyers for the guilty parties awaiting sentence. (Cf Appendix 1 – page 172)

On the front row of the public benches is a pretty but heavily pregnant teenager (17 or 18 years old) called LEONIE. She looks tense and very uncomfortable in these surroundings.

Impressionistic extracts of various cases, perhaps a mixture of information presented at court, and flashback to moments of the incident in question. Along the following lines:

The Sheriff now addresses Albert, the youth from the station. Albert stands on the dock – and by his face it is obvious he has been told off regularly since the day he was born.

SHERIFF

It seems to me, young man, your profound
stupidity is only matched by your good
fortune... [confusion on Albert's face]... I
sentence you to 180 hours of community
service. If you don't carry out the required
work you will come back before me and
receive a custodial sentence... is that clear?

Albert shakes his head. Sheriff holds his head in frustration as the
accused's lawyer walks over to explain.

TITLES

ANGELS' SHARE

Sense of ritual: names called, pale faces with nervous eyes, some
lost, confused, frightened, while others seem just so defeated they
don't care. Name, stand, sit, stare, a litany of the crushed.

CUT TO ANOTHER CASE:

A young woman, MO, around 20, with nervous, darting eyes, and
fast fingers twiddling on the stand before her, stands in the dock.
Dressed in trackie bottoms, and daft top (with Spider-Man on the
front) she looks as tough as nails, and chews chewing gum. (On
her right hand and stretching up her wrist she has a spider's web
and Spider-Man tattooed.)

SHERIFF CLERK

Are you Maureen Stone?

MO

[Nickname Mo] Aye...

The court officer beside whispers aggressively in her ear.

MO (CONT'D)
Yes, yer Honourship!

SHERIFF
Are you chewing gum young lady?

Mo swallows it in a gulp.

MO
Naw.

Again, the Sheriff shakes his head as he stares at the accused.

CUT TO THE FISCAL IN MID-NARRATIVE:

FISCAL
The accused stole a yellow and blue macaw
from a pet shot in the Gallogate area of the
city… it had a market value of 1,800 pounds…
it is quite a hefty bird My Lord, with a wing
span of some five feet…

SHERIFF
Yes, I'm aware of what it looks like…

FISCAL
The bird was stuffed inside a Marks and
Spencers carrier bag with tail protruding…
On being asked for an explanation by a police
constable the accused replied, 'Why don't you
piss off and start hunting rapists, mass murderers
and perverts ya grumpy twat.'

Mo has a twinkle in her eye as she looks out at her friends on the
public benches.

SHERIFF
Was she under the influence of alcohol?

FISCAL

No My Lord, it appears she was fascinated by
the colourful plumage...

SHERIFF

Was it from the Amazonian rainforest?

FISCAL

[Checking her papers] Wigan, My Lord...

More faces. More snippets of narrative.

A young woman, SUSAN, now stands in the dock. Embarrassed,
she stares at her hands.

SHERIFF CLERK

Are you Susan McGovern?

FISCAL

The accused had a part-time cleaning job, My
Lord, three mornings a week and during this
time she continued to claim Social Security
benefits...

An older washed out man, MELLOWS, broken, around fifty, but
looks like well into his sixties, is slouched in the dock.

DEFENCE LAWYER

It seems clear that this offence was committed
not out of any sense of mindless vandalism, but
unfortunately through depression... he wanted
to get back inside the prison system again...

Another young man in a suit stands in the dock. He looks totally
embarrassed and it is quite clear by his accent that he is from a
different part of town.

SHERIFF CLERK

Are you Matthew Bains?

MATTHEW

Yes, that's correct.

DEFENCE LAWYER

My client is in his third year at Glasgow University where he is studying neurology… this is his first offence in an otherwise exemplary record to date. Needless to say extracting his father's luxury Mercedes from a bunker in their local golf course, especially since he was driving without insurance, has left my client deeply apologetic, and highly embarrassed… he hasn't consumed alcohol since that day…

Another tough face.

SHERIFF

A premeditated vicious assault for no apparent reason. I sentence you to 12 months in prison.

SHERIFF CLERK

Call Eamon Mathieson. [Nickname, Rhino]

RHINO, a big solid clumsy lad moves slowly and deliberately towards the dock.

3. FLASHBACK TO GLASGOW CITY CENTRE

Rhino, totally pissed (but not aggressive) with bare chest, hairy as hell, sits on top of a bronze horse statue. Both horse and man have a traffic cone over their heads. A policeman stands below the statue and tries to persuade him to come down. Rhino grabs the traffic cone from his head and puts it to his mouth.

RHINO

[Through traffic cone] If yi promise... hands
on heart... to bring me hame... call it quits...
Ah'll come doon... over and out...

He now sticks the cone to his ear for the response.

POLICEMAN

Straight home... to a warm bath and a cup of
cocoa... look, here's your driver...

The driver of the van appears. The constable is exceptionally tall
and skinny, and it is obvious that he and Rhino have had many a
friendly chat on the meaning of life on previous occasions.

RHINO

[Top of his voice, through the cone, to the
tune of 'Guantanamera'] '...Big wankin'
Beanpole!... Yes a big wankin' Beanpole...
big wanking Beanpole... [deep hammed
up trembling bass] Oh yes a big wankin'
Beanpole!!'

Others standing by are howling with laughter, which doesn't
improve the mood of the tall gent.

COURT:

SHERIFF CLERK

Call Robert Emmerson.

ROBBIE enters from the cells below and is handcuffed to a police
officer. He is brought to the dock and his cuffs are taken from him.
Robbie Emmerson, 20 or so, but with a lifetime on his face. He is
lean, hard, and has a wound-up energy about him. He has a long
scar on the left side of his cheek which disfigures his handsome
face.

23

He catches sight of Leonie in the front row. Her eyes fill and she puts her hand nervously to her mouth.

Several of the youngsters in the public gallery come to life as Robbie takes up his position in the dock. One individual in particular, CLANCY, a tough looking youth stares at him with barely controlled fury. He mouths the words 'you're fucking dead' together with a gesture of his finger across his throat. It only encourages his sidekick, an aggressive youth called SNIPER (with distinctive tattoo coming up from under his shirt and onto neck) who gives Robbie the middle finger.

Robbie ignores them and stares out at the court. But it upsets Leonie even more. There is something very different about Robbie from those that have gone before. He has spirit, poise and sense of himself that projects itself from the dock.

> SHERIFF CLERK (CONT'D)
> Are you Robert Emmerson?

> ROBBIE
> 'Robbie' Emmerson.

The Sheriff eyes him up.

> FISCAL
> I would accept that the accused's rival in this case provoked the entire incident, but at the same time, the severity and the viciousness of the accused's reaction went far and beyond self-defence… both of the accused's rivals… [Clancy and Sniper, mouthing insults under their breath, stare at him from the public gallery] were assaulted to their severe and permanent disfigurement and both required hospital attention…

DEFENCE LAWYER

My client's record is deplorable, but perhaps
given his chaotic childhood, and the fact that
both his parents were in and out of custody, he
didn't have the best start in life. You will notice
from the report My Lord that since being
released from Polmont Young Offenders, the
last ten months have been trouble free apart
from this one very serious incident. He is a
very determined and intelligent young man.
He makes job applications on a daily basis.
His young girlfriend has been a very positive
influence on his life; the reason is clear – within
ten days he will become a father.

Leonie stares at him from the public benches.

DEFENCE LAWYER VOICE OVER

If he receives a custodial sentence today he will
miss the birth of his child. The prospects of
fatherhood have changed this young man, and
he would grasp one last opportunity with both
hands...

The defence lawyer sits down.

SHERIFF

[Flicking through the report, reflecting] He has
clashed on several occasions with his girlfriend's
father which gives rise to serious concern... he
is banned from the house in which she lives...

There is silence for some moments as the Sheriff reads more of
the background report.

Leonie is even more stressed out.

SHERIFF (CONT'D)

Robbie Emmerson. Stand up. Your record is
appalling. For much of your short life you have
behaved like a thug, and the violent incidents
in this case have proven to me that you are still
a very dangerous individual.

Leonie looks devastated.

SHERIFF (CONT'D)

But you are obviously a young man with
energy and talent. You have escaped a significant
custodial sentence by the skin of your teeth.

CLANCY

[From the benches] Fuckin' joke man...

SHERIFF CLERK

Silence in court!

SHERIFF

Is your client prepared to carry out 300 hours
of community service?

Robbie's eyes flash at Leonie as he lets out a breath of relief.

LAWYER

He is My Lord... and I know he will be very
grateful for this opportunity.

SHERIFF

And so he should be... it is his last chance.

4. OUTSIDE THE SHERIFF COURT

Robbie and Leonie, hand in hand, make their way down the steps from the court building and move over to the wall overlooking the river Clyde.

> ROBBIE
> Fuck... Ah canni believe it...

Leonie bursts out crying. They cling on to each other. She continues to sob.

> ROBBIE (CONT'D)
> It's okay Leonie... it's okay...

> LEONIE
> My God... I thought he was going to put yi
> away for years...

She starts to sob even more. He tenderly touches her bump.

> ROBBIE
> Hey... a' that jigglin' aboot... yi'll end up in
> labour... Ah don't want ma son born on the
> steps of a sheriff court!

Leonie starts to giggle through her sobs. And then she changes again. She looks up at the imposing court, the clusters of the accused and families outside, and the chatting lawyers in their gowns out for a smoke. It really gets her. She sees an older women, heartbroken, being comforted by family members and friends. She puts her hand protectively over her tummy.

> LEONIE
> I'll never come here again Robbie... I'm tellin'
> yi now...

ROBBIE

Leonie… it's over…

LEONIE

Look at me… one more time and yi'll be on
your own… I'll cut you off.

She means it. He gives her a hug, and he looks beyond her up to
the facade of the court once more.

Clancy and Sniper (from the public benches) and three of their
mates (heavy-duty toughs) walk down the steps at speed and
confront Robbie who instinctively stands in front of Leonie to
protect her.

CLANCY

Think it's over… Yi wid have been safer inside
ya prick…

SNIPER

At every corner… we'll be waitin'…

They walk off. It upsets Leonie even more.

LEONIE

I canni live wi this Robbie… and I'm no goin'
to…

5. COMMUNITY SERVICE – EARLY MORNING

Two passenger vans that hold about a dozen each are parked in a
suitable picking-up point in Glasgow's East End.

There are two supervisors (each in charge of a van) who tick
off the names of those arriving to do their community service.
HARRY, (in his early fifties, a joiner by trade who ran his own
little building company before) a warm engaging presence, who

has the knack of taking the heat out of a situation, is in charge of one van. JEAN, a woman in her early fifties too, ex-prison officer, takes charge of the other.

[Harry has a generous streak that the 'service users' quickly recognise. He has recently come to the job and isn't burnt out. He wants them to get through their hours, but also, if possible learn something on the way. He is of a generation accustomed to work. He has had a job every day of his life since 16. He can turn his hand to most things; market gardening, landscaping, fixing his own car. He has a real hinterland to him. He even once built his own house. He has read books, enjoys food, drink and music. But he also has his secret passion which he got from his father who worked in the Highlands before coming to the city.]

The motley crew arrive and are ticked off one by one; there are around 15 of them and they are divided up between the two vans. This will include some of the faces from court above. Rhino (statue) Mo (theft of bird) Albert (railway track) Matthew (the student) Susan (social security fraud) and another 4 or 5 young women.

Albert approaches Harry.

ALBERT

Albert Ridley.

Harry searches through his list.

HARRY

Yi're no on the list Albert...

ALBERT

The fucking judge dude put me specially on
the list... got to be there...

This causes some amusement among the others.

HARRY

No sign... sure it was today?

ALBERT

Is this Wednesday?

HARRY

Just two days out... but Ah'll tell you what...
if you can tell me whit year it is, Ah'll let you
come?

Albert tries to remember...

HARRY (CONT'D)

Never mind... Ah'm two bodies short... Ah'll
need your talent to paint the community
centre...

Jean the other supervisor hears this and laughs to herself.

Matthew, nervous and uncomfortable, arrives and the others notice
he is different immediately.

MATTHEW

Matthew Baines...

The others pounce on the accent immediately and start to take
the piss.

RHINO

Bingo! A posh cunt... whit did yi dae... no
finish yer homework? Shag the butler?

JEAN

Right cut out that language boys... we have
ladies present...

MO

But he is a posh cunt! Listen tae him.

HARRY

Right you can call him 'PC', but cut out that
nasty stuff eh?

This takes the heat out of it and they laugh.

ALBERT

[Shaking his hand] Hey PC… you're the man!

Jean confronts a man in his thirties who is obviously on drugs or
drunk or both.

MAN

Willy's the name…

JEAN

Your surname, Willy?

MAN

That's private…

JEAN

You've been drinking Willy… can't take you
under the influence… you'll have to come
another day mate… on you go Willy…

MAN

Hivnie had a drink a' mornin…

HARRY

Come on guys… into the van, that's us. Get
your calls done now… strictly no mobiles
during work… let's go, we're runnin' late…

Jean's van drives off.

Just as Harry's van is about to pull out, Robbie, out of breath,
sprints up to Harry and tries to get on the van.

ROBBIE

Wait! Open the door...

HARRY

Yi should have been here at 8.00 sharp... it's no a taxi service...

ROBBIE

Bus sailed right past me...

HARRY

Fifteen minutes late... that's the cut-off... sorry son...

ROBBIE

[Urgent] Ah've got tae git ma hoors done man... please...

Harry hesitates for a moment.

HARRY

At least yi're keen... jump in...

ROBBIE

[Eyes lighting up] Thanks man...

6. COMMUNITY CENTRE

Harry and Jean are in the process of organising the gang into teams to paint the community centre, which has various rooms, corridors and halls.

Generally the more competent ones (including Robbie and PC) are given ladders and long rollers for the highest parts of the walls, while the less co-ordinated are given simpler jobs at ground level. They are all full of cheek and backchat but Harry and Jean take it all in their stride.

There is a sense of Harry enjoying the work with the gang, as well as taking on the challenge of getting them to do a good job too.

> HARRY
>
> Right come on guys... this place is used by everyone from toddlers to pensioners... we're going to do a right professional job on this and really cheer them up... something we can be proud of.

ROOM AND CORRIDOR: To Albert and another even more dopey lad.

> HARRY (CONT'D)
>
> Have you ever painted before?

> ALBERT
>
> Just wi a can...

The other boy shakes his head.

> HARRY
>
> [Handing the quiet one a brush] Right Rembrandt... for you... try and finish the wall before the break... and don't forget the windows... think you can manage?

Albert and partner, brushes at the ready, stare at the challenge ahead.

ANOTHER SPOT: Robbie is already at work with a roller. He paints with coordination and rhythm at three times the speed of the others as if trying to burn up excess energy.

Mellows (older washed-out man from court) slowly stirs his paint.

Harry lays down a can of paint beside Rhino and PC.

RHINO

Fuck sake Harry… Ah hate this colour…

HARRY

My apologies Rhino… Ah'll get the interior
designer to consult you next time…

Rhino and PC are given a wall to do opposite Robbie.

MELLOWS

[To Robbie] Slow down yi prick…

ROBBIE

[Quietly, into his face] Ah'll treat you polite…
you dae the same… got that Mister? Ah just
want to git through this… wi nae hassle.

Mellows backs off at the sizzling vigour underneath. Robbie goes
back to painting, but even faster this time.

Harry and Jean watch him streak through his work for a minute
or two till something else catches their attention and makes them
smile.

RHINO

The birds up that uni… must be some randy
little dolls up there eh?

PC just looks down at him, unable to answer. Mo shakes her head
and catches Jean's eye.

RHINO (CONT'D)

Neurology eh?… Must be somethin' tae dae wi
nature?

PC

With neurons.

34

Rhino holds the ladder for PC who stretches into the far corner with the roller.

                    RHINO
        So what exactly is a neuron?

A moment's silence.

                    MO
        You should know… rhymes wi moron…

Rhino looks up at a group of them giggling at him.

                    RHINO
        Ah'm no a fuckin' moron by the way…

ANOTHER SPOT: Jean chats with Susan (social security case) as they both stir pots of paint.

                    JEAN
        How was the job interview?

                    SUSAN
        Ah wuz so nervous but the man said Ah was
        great… 'a leadin' candidate' he said… he even
        shook ma hand…

                    JEAN
        That's fantastic Susan… when will yi hear?

                    SUSAN
        [Shrugging] Been ten days noo… [stirring]
        the secretary told me there were ower four
        hundred applications… only forty got an
        interview… but yi hiv tae stay positive… hivn't
        yi?

IN THE CORRIDOR: Harry and Jean stand staring at the wall with Albert and the other boy. They genuinely look proud of their work. It is more than irregular – thick at some points, sparse in others, with several superficial streaks interspersed by long thick 'tears' dripping down from the top.

> JEAN
> No bad for the first time boys…

> HARRY
> [Appreciating] Kind o' Jackson Pollock… if this was in a New York museum you guys wid be millionaires…

> ALBERT
> Ah'll hire yi as ma agent Harry.

Harry's mobile rings. His face changes colour.

> HARRY
> Bloody hell!… Take him up there? Are yi sure? Okay, I'll ask Jean to cover for me. What's her name?

Harry rushes through to where Robbie is still painting.

> HARRY (CONT'D)
> Leonie is in labour… Come on, Ah'll take you to the hospital.

7. VAN TO HOSPITAL

Robbie sits on the passenger side. He methodically goes through every pocket in his trousers, back and front, counting up every penny. He then starts on his jacket, inside, outside, top and bottom. It is clear he hasn't got much. Harry glances at him.

ROBBIE

Got tae buy some flewers…

He counts out the total to himself and then puts it all in his jacket pocket. They drive on in silence for a few moments.

ROBBIE (CONT'D)

Can Ah ask yi a big favour?

Harry turns to look at him.

ROBBIE (CONT'D)

Can yi come in wi me?

HARRY

Why… what's wrong?

ROBBIE

Ah'm scared they won't let me in…

HARRY

Are you sure Leonie wants you there?

ROBBIE

One hundred per cent. Want tae see her text?

Harry hesitates.

ROBBIE (CONT'D)

They just take one look at ma face…

Harry glances at him once more.

8. HOSPITAL, STAIRS AND CORRIDOR

Robbie (carrying a simple bunch of flowers) and Harry walk up a set of stairs and come out into a corridor that leads to the birthing suites. They move towards a room, but Robbie spots a few men in the distance. A tough, burly man in his mid-forties (MATT,

Leonie's father) and his two equally weighty brothers are standing outside the room where Leonie is. They spot him and are on the move immediately.

ROBBIE
Fuck… Leonie's Da.

The three men don't stop and head straight for Robbie. Matt glances round the corridor, and smiles as he gets closer.

MATT
Good to see yi wee man… been expecting you
to show up…

He puts his arms round Robbie's shoulder as he and the two brothers sweep him though a door to the emergency stairs in a false wave of bonhomie.

They totally ignore Harry, who is slightly confused. Harry follows them. He is taken aback by their speed and directness as they bundle Robbie down towards the exit.

ROBBIE
Will you listen tae me… Leonie wants me
here…

HARRY
Hey, guys! Will you please calm down…

Harry might as well not exist.

Once into the stairs, Robbie struggles and the flowers get trampled.

ROBBIE
Let me speak for Christ's sake… Leonie just
sent me a text…

MATT

Show me the phone...

The two brothers let Robbie take out his phone.

ROBBIE

Ah don't want any hassle... just let me in tae
see her...

Matt takes the phone but instead of checking the message he
drops it to the ground and stamps it to pieces as the other two
men grab Robbie again.

ROBBIE (CONT'D)

Ah've got a right to be there!

Matt viciously headbutts Robbie smack in the face and punches
him powerfully in the solar plexus. He drops to the ground.

HARRY

Jesus... cool it! Calm down...

Harry is violently pushed away up against the wall and knows he
can't intervene physically.

MATT

Fuck all rights... Yer Da was a prick... yer
brother's a prick... and you're a prick! A long
line of scumbag losers and it stops here. If Ah
see yi within a mile of Leonie Ah'll hiv yer
baws cut aff!

ROBBIE

It's ma baby too...

This infuriates Matt who boots him repeatedly so hard it totally
winds Robbie who struggles to breathe. He then bends down and
grabs him by the lapels. Face to face.

MATT

You are nuthin to this baby. Nuthin! Git that
through yer thick skull once and for all or Ah
swear Ah'll hiv yi done…

He turns to face Harry and gets right up to his face.

MATT (CONT'D)

You know fuck all… keep yer fat nose tae
yersel, arsehole.

They march back towards the corridor and leave them there.

Harry tries to help Robbie to his feet but he is still winded. He
sits up against the wall as he coughs. Harry picks up the remnants
of the smashed mobile.

Robbie pulls himself up against the wall. He begins to recover.

ROBBIE

Ah'm gonni fucking do him…

He makes to run up the stairs past Harry. Harry grabs him.

HARRY

Just what they want… you behind bars for the
next ten years…

ROBBIE

Let me at him! Fuck off Harry!

Harry still blocks his way and hangs onto him.

HARRY

Are you going to let them win so easily? Eh?
Never see your baby… ever!

This gets Robbie and he stops struggling. A moment between
them.

Harry leads Robbie towards a toilet on the way out of the hospital.

INSIDE: Harry grabs several paper towels, steeps them in cold water and puts them to Robbie's swollen and cut cheek.

Close up, Harry can see several scars on Robbie's face.

                    HARRY (CONT'D)
        Hold that... bring down the swelling...

Robbie, still raw, but more composed, examines his options as he presses the towels to the wound and confronts his own image in the mirror.

                    ROBBIE
        She's got tae feel calm... if she sees me like
        this... she'll git distressed... canni believe Ah'll
        miss the birth...

Harry feels for him.

                    HARRY
        We could call the police... Ah can help yi
        explain...

                    ROBBIE
        Naw... we didnae dae that... ever.

There is a finality to it, and Harry doesn't push. Harry gives him fresh paper towels for the cut above his brow.

                    HARRY
        Where dae yi live Robbie?

                    ROBBIE
        Depends... sofa hoppin' between mates...
        trying to git a place on my ain...

HARRY

Right… let's get a bite to eat at ma place… yi
can clean up proper and calm down…

ROBBIE

Fuck! He smashed ma phone…

Harry watches him for a moment and hands him his own mobile.

HARRY

Why don't yi text Leonie?

ROBBIE

Thanks Harry…

9. STREET AND INTO HARRY'S FLAT

The van, with Harry and Robbie, turns off Duke Street, in the
East End of Glasgow, towards Harry's rented flat. (He lives in
Dennistoun. It is a Victorian building, but modest. He has put effort
into making it optimistic. Good taste, without being over done.)

LATER: Harry and Robbie eat in the kitchen. Harry has prepared
a simple but delicious pasta.

Harry's phone is between them, on the table.

Harry studies him (taking in the scar) for some moments as
Robbie wolfs down his food. It makes him smile to see Robbie
relish it so.

His face has ugly bruising and the swelling is still obvious.

HARRY

Looks a sore one… are yi okay?

ROBBIE

Nuthin… a wee scratch…

He goes back to his plate, swiping up the sauce with some bread.

HARRY

What's her dad do?

ROBBIE

Can you no guess?

HARRY

A librarian?

Robbie chuckles.

ROBBIE

Him and his brithers run a couple o' bars in the
East End… make a fortune… fucking hated me
since the first day… then he found oot Ah gave
him a nickname which stuck… didnae help
much when someone sprayed a' over his fancy
motor…

HARRY

Which was?

ROBBIE

'Psycho Baws!!'

Harry just chuckles. Robbie polishes off the last of the sauce.

ROBBIE (CONT'D)

But her mam's cool… she likes me, but duznie
git much say… That wuz good… thank you.

Robbie has a habit of looking a person in the eye – and he does
the same with Harry.

ROBBIE (CONT'D)

Nice pad… is yir family aboot?

Harry hesitates for a moment.

HARRY

No… Ah live here on ma own…

ROBBIE

Yi'r no an oul poof are yi?

Harry chuckles.

HARRY

Just spiked yer drink… Not every day yi have
your first child is it?

Robbie stares at him.

ROBBIE

Have you got kids?

HARRY

Two grown up girls… down south…

ROBBIE

Are yis close?

Again that direct look.

The phone begins to buzz and then vibrate across the table. Their
eyes flash at each other. Harry leaves it to Robbie. Robbie picks
it up and recognises the number. He looks stunned and almost
scared to answer.

HARRY

Go on! Take it through to the sitting room…
go on!

Robbie goes through to the other room and heads to the window
and stares outside as he feels his future flash in front of him. Still
it rings. At last he answers.

LEONIE

Seven pounds fourteen ounces…

ROBBIE

Leonie!

LEONIE

He's so beautiful Robbie…

ROBBIE

A son…

LEONIE

He's perfect… our wee man… he's got
gorgeous blue eyes… just like yours…

He struggles to control himself.

ROBBIE

Sorry fir no being there darlin'… so sorry…
they wouldnie let me pass…

LEONIE

I know what happened… don't fret… don't
fret Robbie… Ma told me everythin'…

ROBBIE

Ah'll make this up to yi… [pause] Can Ah
come up?

LEONIE

Da's still here with ma Ma… I'm sorry… love
you Robbie… got to go… here's the doctor…
he wants to examine him… phone yi later…

Robbie turns off the phone and leans his head on the window.

ROBBIE

Fuckin' hell…

Harry tentatively appears at the door.

HARRY

Okay?

ROBBIE

A wee boy… canni believe it…

HARRY

Congratulations Robbie!… This calls for
something special.

Harry, with Robbie beside him, opens a cupboard to reveal packed
shelves filled up with bottles of single malt whisky. The bottles look
magical as if each carries its own secret. Different shapes, colours,
and even the labels look exotic. Some are in tins or decorated
boxes. The names too are somehow mysterious and other-worldly.

Harry handles each bottle reverently, delicately… thinking.
Picking out one – a tall thin bottle (but with only 35cl, approx
half bottle) and wiping the dust off it.

ROBBIE

Whisky… never even tasted it…

HARRY

Ah! Got this as a present years ago…
[Hesitating, glancing at Robbie] What the
hell… now or never… Springbank… 32 years
old!… [Opening the full bottle for the first
time, catching the aromas] Oh my God… a
toast for your first born Robbie…

He fishes out two delicate 'nosing' glasses and gently pours out
the golden nectar as he talks.

HARRY (CONT'D)

[As he pours he savours the colour too] Our
most delicate and intimate organ… [pause] the
humble nose…

He puts his hand over the glass and shakes up the drink vigorously
for a second or two.

HARRY (CONT'D)

Better smelling it than tasting it… get to know
and respect your honker Robbie…

Robbie chuckles.

Harry sniffs the glass and almost goes into rapture. Robbie tries
the same and then coughs.

Harry now holds up the glass to the light and swirls the whisky
round again. Robbie copies and studies his glass against the light.

HARRY (CONT'D)

See how it runs down the side of the glass…
we call those 'tears' or 'legs'… right… what's
his name?

ROBBIE

Luke… his name is Luke.

HARRY

Well… here's to Luke… and his 'old man'.

ROBBIE

To ma son Luke. Happy birthday…

They both chink glasses and take a taste.

Harry is in seventh heaven while Robbie coughs.

ROBBIE (CONT'D)

No offence Harry… but tastes like shite! Can
Ah mix it wi coke?

HARRY

Barbarian numbskull… Try it now with a little
water… [He adds a little water to both glasses]
Luke… good name… after your old man?

ROBBIE

No way.

Robbie sips again. It isn't so strong; a hint of curiosity aroused.

ROBBIE (CONT'D)

Fuck's sake… Ah'm a Da.

Harry studies his young face, scrawny build, and senses his spirit.

HARRY

[Taking the phone] Now… got tae speak tae
the sister who runs the ward… see if she'll let
yi in tae see yer son…

ROBBIE

Jesus Harry… too late… they'll never let me
in…

HARRY

Where there's a will… there's a way.

Robbie's eyes shine at the possibility.

10. HOSPITAL – NIGHT

Robbie walks along the corridor clutching a bunch of flowers.
Tentatively, he approaches the nursing area, and moves towards a
mature nurse.

SISTER

Are you Robbie?

He nods sheepishly.

SISTER (CONT'D)

This is a total exception... lucky she's in a
room to herself... [indicating]... half an hour...
[softening]... he's a wee beauty...

Robbie enters the room, which has three beds, but only one
occupied.

Leonie, sitting up, smiles at him as he offers her the flowers and
gives her a little kiss.

ROBBIE

Are you okay?

She nods, but he can tell it was painful.

He looks across at the cot with baby Luke. Leonie is beaming.
Robbie moves closer and stares down at his child. He is stunned.

LEONIE

Are yi going to pick up your son?

ROBBIE

Can Ah?

She chuckles.

Robbie tenderly picks him up and just stares at him for some time.
He gently touches his cheek, his nose, and then is fascinated by his
tiny hand which grips his finger. He smells him. He gently bends
his forehead down to touch Luke's.

LEONIE

Well... are yi going to say something?

Robbie is overcome. He can't speak. He hugs the baby in his arms, stands up, moves to the window and turns his back to Leonie. She can see his entire body shake with silent sobs.

She moves over to him and cuddles him and Luke from behind without saying anything.

15 MINUTES LATER: A shirt is thrown down onto the bed.

Robbie sits down, barechested on a seat by the bed as Leonie passes a naked baby Luke into Robbie's hands. Robbie lays Luke on his chest.

[Leonie notices the stab and slash wounds on Robbie's side, long since stitched, but still leaving their angry red marks.]

Robbie is nearly overcome again by the tenderness of the moment.

ROBBIE
[Whispering] Oh my God…

LEONIE
He loves the heat… and your heartbeat… he's
used to mine from being inside me…

ROBBIE
Ah Leonie…

He can barely continue. He kisses Luke's head and tenderly strokes his back. Leonie snuggles in close to them both.

ROBBIE (CONT'D)
'Luke'… I love the sound o' his name…
Luke…

She nods and smiles.

LEONIE

Me too… The midwife told me only half his
brain has developed… the next half depends
on us.

He looks up at her and can see the challenge in her eye.

LEONIE (CONT'D)

He'll only get one shot at being a baby
Robbie… one. You know what that means…
don't you?

Robbie kisses his head once more as he cuddles him tight.

11. STREET AND STAIRS TO DOUGIE'S FLAT – NIGHT

By Hamiltonhill, near Possil on the north side of Glasgow. Robbie
walks past council house flats, some of which are boarded-up.

Robbie enters the close and climbs up the stairs. (They are scruffy,
and covered in graffiti and a few of the doors are boarded up too.)

He hesitates outside an apartment door. He can hear ear-splitting
music and sounds of voices of youngsters horsing around inside.
He sighs to himself as he fumbles for his keys.

He puts the key in the lock. More shrieks from inside. He can't
face them. He extracts the keys, and sits down on the steps by
himself.

He leans his head against the wall and closes his eyes, as the music
thumps on from inside.

Suddenly the door bursts open. DOUGIE, his flatmate, pale-faced,
emaciated, and clutching a colossal 3-litre bottle of cider stares
down at him.

DOUGIE

Been waitin' on yi… git in here and get tore
in… party time!

Robbie just looks up at him.

DOUGIE (CONT'D)

Fuckin' misery guts… come on… a wee drink
will cheer yi up man…

Dougie plonks himself down beside him, swings an arm over his
shoulder, and offers him the enormous container.

ROBBIE

No thanks Dougie… no in the mood man.

12. SPIRES PARK, ROYSTON HILL, GLASGOW

An old ruined church gives some privacy from the main street to
a little park overlooking the city. It is a secluded spot which gives
Robbie and Leonie more security to meet.

Robbie, with baby Luke in a Wilkinet (pouch) on his chest, sits
beside Leonie on a park bench.

Robbie peers into Luke's eyes and perhaps rubs his nose against
his as he plays with him.

Leonie, worried, reads from a letter. At last she looks up.

LEONIE

What does 'TASC' mean?

ROBBIE

'Talk After Serious Crime.'

She folds up the letter and hands it back to Robbie who places
it in his pocket.

LEONIE

Is that the one you went to prison for... the
boy you really hurt?

He nods.

ROBBIE

Fuck... whit dae they want tae meet me fir?

LEONIE

[Gentle] Maybe it helps the boy and his family
deal with it... cope wi the past... that's the idea
isn't it?

Robbie looks ashamed, stressed, and stares at his hands.

LEONIE (CONT'D)

I think you owe them...

ROBBIE

Served ma fucking time...

LEONIE

And what about them Robbie? Do they count?

He can't answer.

LEONIE (CONT'D)

I think you should go... might help you too?

Silence.

LEONIE (CONT'D)

Are yi scared to face them... or scared to face
yersel?

This gets to him.

LEONIE (CONT'D)

Do you want me to come with you?

Robbie stares at her for a moment. She can spot his confusion and need for support.

> ROBBIE
> Yi'r gonni be disgusted…

Robbie looks down.

> ROBBIE (CONT'D)
> [Quietly] Yi might hate me Leonie…

Leonie takes Luke's hand and holds it tenderly.

> LEONIE
> Look at me… [he looks up] Are we in this
> together or not?

13. LOCAL AUTHORITY MEETING ROOM

Several people sit round a table. Robbie, with Leonie by his side holding Luke, sit at one side of the table. The atmosphere is electric as a young man, ANTHONY, aged around 23, accompanied by his MOTHER, FATHER, and younger SISTER, sit on the other side of the table.

A MODERATOR sits between them to keep the meeting calm, peaceful and to the terms previously discussed and agreed between the parties.

The young man, Anthony, nervous, and highly upset recalls the incident in question.

His family members also struggle to control their emotions as they listen to his shocking memories.

Robbie stares between his hands and at Anthony. He appears cold, uncaring and expressionless.

Leonie, increasingly distressed and shocked, pays close attention as the facts unfold.

The lad hesitates, struggling to go on.

> ANTHONY
> I was just trying to park the car… it was a tight space and the back wheel must have mounted the pavement by about three inches… next thing there was this guy cursing and swearing at us like a total madman… he came at us from nowhere… 'Fucking areshole… fucking prick… who the fuck do you think you are in your big fucking motor!'

> MODERATOR
> Take your time Anthony… it's okay…

14. FLASHBACK – CITY CENTRE STREET – EVENING

Robbie, and a few other youths walk along the street. Robbie, almost three years younger, with his hair quite different, appears under the influence of drugs and alcohol. He looks dangerous and unpredictable.

Just as he walks along, totally by coincidence, a mid-range but stylish new car reverses into a parking space by the pavement. The back wheel mounts the pavement by a few inches.

Robbie turns to stare. Inside he sees a fresh faced handsome young lad, around 20, driving the car. He's in conversation with his very attractive girlfriend. It looks like she has made a joke at his bad driving and the lad laughs as he tries to continue the manoeuvre.

Robbie stares at them for a few seconds and then explodes. He starts pounding and kicking the car terrifying the two youngsters inside. The car stalls. In a second he has jumped over the bonnet to get at the driver's side. He pulls open the door and drags the young lad out by the hair as his girlfriend screams…

> ANTHONY'S VOICE OVER
> Grabbed me by the hair… couldn't break his grip… next thing he dragged me out and started punching me… then smashing my head against the ground… I was begging him to stop… so was Ann… she was in bits… he just wouldn't stop.

BACK TO THE ROOM:
Leonie, stunned, turns to look at Robbie who stares ahead impassively.

> ANTHONY
> I thought 'he's going to kill me… that's it'.

Tears roll down Leonie's cheeks as she cuddles into Luke.

> ANTHONY (CONT'D)
> Police told me later he had been on 'Buckfast and Blues', like a zombie… I woke up in hospital… two broken fingers and a cracked wrist… one side of my head had been completely shaved and I had twelve stitches along one side… the surgeon said I was lucky… very lucky… he told me then I had a detached retina and lost the sight in my left eye…

Leonie can't help but sob into herself.

> ANTHONY (CONT'D)
> [Hesitation, looking up at Robbie] I don't know you… never seen you before… I never

did anything to you... didn't insult or provoke
you...Why did you hurt me like this... for no
reason... Why?

Robbie looks up at every eye upon him. Including a devastated
Leonie.

LATER:

>   MOTHER
> When I saw him... [pause]... his head were so
> swollen I thought 'my son is going to die'...

She struggles to go on. Anthony puts his hand over his mother's.
Robbie and Leonie notice both hands tremble.

>   MOTHER (CONT'D)
> The drip, the tubes, the monitors... it was all
> too much... it was very difficult after Anthony
> came back from the hospital... he just wanted
> to be in his room, alone... the toughest thing
> of all was to see this wonderful easy going
> young man totally lose confidence in himself...
> [she struggles to control herself]... we couldn't
> get him out of the house even after his hair
> grew in... He dropped out of college... lost his
> girlfriend... lost his spirit... Shona his youngest
> sister... she was so broken-hearted she failed
> her exams... my husband... [she turns to look
> at him and his head drops] is a different man...
> he blamed himself for giving Anthony the
> new car and he wondered if that had been the
> spark for the attack... I keep having the same
> nightmare... that you attack him again and
> again and again...

Leonie can't control a sudden sob, and then flashes a dark look at Robbie. The mother struggles to go on but is determined to finish.

> MOTHER (CONT'D)
>
> I've read about people like you in the newspaper... I have tried to put you out of my mind... [shaking her head] I've wondered who you are?... [looking at him] Are you just an ignorant thug... or do you realise you have torn our family apart?... My oldest son has lost the sight in his eye... I don't even care if you are sorry or not... I just want to ask you one question... Do you understand the damage you have caused?

Robbie looks at his hands again.

> MOTHER (CONT'D)
>
> Look at me... will you wreck another family?

Silence.

Leonie stares at Robbie desperately.

> LEONIE
>
> [Furious and ashamed] Robbie... say something... say sorry...

> MODERATOR
>
> Robbie... would you like to answer?

Robbie looks up at her. Then at the father, who looks like he is ready to pounce. He looks at the young sister who has tears in her eyes. Still the mother, with her bright intelligent eyes, stares at him, waiting for an answer. Robbie's gaze flashes between mother and son. Anthony takes his mother's hand. Robbie can see their hands tremble again.

Robbie... we have talked about this... you volunteered to come here... would you like to say something?

Robbie's eyes drop again and he stares at his hands.

FATHER

[Jumping up, leaving] I'm sorry... got to get out of here... your sentence is over... that's what gets me... we have a life sentence you evil little bastard!

He marches out and slams the door in a fury.

Robbie looks at the mother again, still staring at him. She gently shakes her head in resignation.

ANTHONY

Sorry Mum... it's been a waste of time.

Leonie, stunned, and heartbroken, begins to sob as Robbie closes down; ice cold.

15. SIMPLE CAFE: HALF HOUR LATER

Leonie brings across two cups of tea and lays them on the table. Robbie, with Luke in his arms, is still stiff and cold. Leonie stares at him.

LEONIE

I felt ashamed... I did...

At last Robbie tries to speak.

ROBBIE

[Struggling] Ah wanted tae tell her something...

He can't continue.

                    LEONIE
        Tell her what?

                    ROBBIE
        [Struggling again] Ah wanted to tell her…
        if someone had done that tae ma son… tae
        Luke… Ah'd want the bastard hung…

He's crushed by shame as Leonie stares at him.

After a moment Robbie turns Luke round to face him. He holds
him tenderly, face to face.

                    ROBBIE (CONT'D)
        Luke… Ah swear on yer life and mine Ah will
        never hurt another person as long as Ah live…

He kisses Luke's forehead.

                    ROBBIE (CONT'D)
        That's a promise…

Leonie continues to look at him for a few moments.

                    LEONIE
        [Whispering] You could have killed him
        Robbie.

                    ROBBIE
        Sounds like Ah did…

Leonie's eyes harden.

                    LEONIE
        What if Clancy suddenly appears… What about
        your promise then? Will you walk away?

ROBBIE

If Ah turn, and take aff... he'll stab me in the back.

LEONIE

What is it between you two?

Robbie struggles to answer.

ROBBIE

His Da fought ma Da... then school, then 'stuff'... been like that fir years... just the way it is...

LEONIE

'Just the way it is'... and will Luke fight his son? [His eyes drop] Look at me!

ROBBIE

It's like we canni break oot... stuck in the loop... scared tae lose face...

LEONIE

In front of who? Thirty little toerags who are as lost as you? [Struggling to understand] A' the struttin', the shoutin', the threats... just like ma Da... like ma brothers... playin' the tough guy... carrying knives and baseball bats and beatin' people up... but inside yi're like frightened wee boys... scared o' the world... [holding his eye] I want you to be a real father to ma child... No a mouse playing the hard man. If no, I'll take care o' Luke masel and make sure he's different...

16. VAN, SCOTTISH COUNTRYSIDE – DAY

FROM OUTSIDE THE VAN:

It is a beautiful summer's day and Harry drives the packed van through stunning Scottish countryside.

Robbie, Mo, Albert, Rhino, Susan and three others are in great form as they speed along.

> HARRY'S VOICE OVER
>
> Ma day aff… if Ah get caught wi you lot in the van Ah'm for the high jump… so repeat after me… 'I do hereby solemnly swear…' repeat it Ah said or you are all walking back!

> GROUP VOICES
>
> 'I do hereby solemnly swear…'

INSIDE THE VAN:

> HARRY
>
> Not to get pissed, rob, fight, or generally cause a rumpus…

> VOICES
>
> [They repeat it] '…or generally cause a rumpus…'

> HARRY
>
> And I further swear… [they repeat] to worship the ground on which big Harry walks…

> VOICES
>
> [Laughter] Fuck off Harry! Where are we going anyway?

> HARRY
>
> Mystery tour… better than the Pyramids and the Coliseum combined…

SUSAN

Tell us Harry!

HARRY

A sacred place…

RHINO

A church?!

HARRY

A distillery ya dumplin! Right hands up…
who's been in the countryside?

He looks in the mirror, not a hand goes up.

HARRY (CONT'D)

Got tae be jokin'!… Right, who's been oot o'
Glasgow?

ROBBIE

Does Polmont count?

They burst out laughing.

One view is more stunning than the other.

LATER: Robbie sits by Harry in the front of the van. They have
a quiet conversation between them as the rest, in the back, joke,
chat and mess around with their mobiles.

ROBBIE (CONT'D)

How many were workin' fir yi?

HARRY

Depended on the project… sometimes up to
twenty… but I had a core of about ten… three
o' them joiners like me… great craftsmen.
Every one.

ROBBIE

So whit happened?

HARRY

We were owed a fortune... last in the chain...
Ah was useless at chasing it up... whole
business just fell apart...

ROBBIE

Twenty-five years up the spout? Lost
everything?

HARRY

Every penny...

ROBBIE

Fuckin' hell... after all that work...

HARRY

Worse for ma missus... a' the stress... the
shame nearly killed her... we lost our home.

ROBBIE

Is she okay now?

HARRY

To be honest Robbie it tore us apart... she's
down south wi one o' ma daughter's... long
story...

ROBBIE

Take's baws tae bounce back... and here yi are
wi scruff bags like us...

Harry smiles to himself and then he looks across at him.

HARRY

You nutters saved my life. Something in the
mornin' tae git up for... we aw need that.

Robbie can see he isn't joking. The van pulls into a lay-by with
an astounding view of the mountains and loch below. There is a
field beside them.

They are all high from the trip and scramble out; like pit ponies
brought to the light.

They are all dying for a piss and the boys head for a gate overlooking
a field.

As Robbie, Rhino, Albert and a few others line up to do their
business they confront a huge shaggy Highland cow with long
horns staring at them from just inside the fence. As they piss...

RHINO

What the hell is that?

ALBERT

Must be a mammoth... Shit, look! [pointing at
the creature] Is that a multiple tadger or whit?

ROBBIE

It's an udder ya twat... a coo's nipples...

RHINO

A bit hairy fir a female... mind you... Ah've
probably shagged worse.

Harry chuckles as he sees Susan and Mo watch the pissing gents
from the back.

SUSAN

Disgusting aren't they?

MO

Whit are we gonni dae?

YOUTH 1

Ah just drap them… we're like a fitba team.

MO

Bloody perverts…

HARRY

Jump the fence… on yi go…

SUSAN

Wi that shaggy beast?!

HARRY

On yi go… it's vegetarian… duznie eat
lassies…

The girls hesitate and begin to climb the fence. Mo jumps over
with a scream and runs over to the side. Susan gets to the top of
the gate, hesitates, and stares at the creature.

SUSAN

No way man… Ah'd rather piss ma pants…

ALBERT

What pants?

SUSAN

Want yer baws wrapped round yer lugs?

ALBERT

Mmm… Ah'm open tae new experiences…

17. A TRADITIONAL DISTILLERY OUTSIDE GLASGOW

A bright-eyed and stunning young woman, MAIRI, in her mid-twenties gives the gang a tour. The boys are hypnotized by her confidence, gift of the gab, knowledge and good looks, the last thing they were expecting in a distillery tour.

> RHINO
>
> [To Harry] Ah thought it wid be some owl'
> bandy sod wi' a kilt man... nae mair vodka fir
> me...

While Mairi gives the main presentation to the group, Harry whispers other points to Robbie who is totally absorbed, way beyond the others.

MALTING FLOOR, STORE ROOM:
Long malting floor supported with pillars. Shafts of light coming in from open windows to pierce the gloom.

> MAIRI
>
> Whisky is made from three simple
> ingredients... water, the purest water, yeast and
> barley... it might sound simple but the process
> is almost magical... part science... part art...
> with an infinity of possibilities... This distillery
> was first licenced in 1824 and is one of the
> oldest independent distilleries in Scotland...
> and it all starts here...

She turns round to face a long long expanse of barley laid out on a traditional malting floor.

> MAIRI (CONT'D)
>
> With locally grown barley...

A couple of workmen walk through the barley which is about three and half inches thick, turning the barley with a wooden shovel called a 'shiel'.

Robbie stoops down to the barley and grabs a handful. He smells it, and then lets it run through his fingers. Harry joins him.

> HARRY
>
> See… it's germinating… it has to be turned to keep cool… [examining the barley close up] see the little shoot… the starch in the grains turns to sugar… which turns into alcohol…

Robbie, captivated, stares at the worker turning the barley.

> ROBBIE
>
> Amazin'…

Harry watches as Robbie wonders over and talks to an older workman who is turning the barley. He hands Robbie the shiel.

BY A KILN: A worker stokes a kiln with peat to dry the barley.

> MAIRI
>
> Roddy stops the germination by drying the barley over the kiln… he's using peat which gives one of our whiskies that distinctive smoky flavour…

> ALBERT
>
> Smoky flavour hersel… wonder if she fancies a wee tour 'roon Carntyne?

Susan turns round and gives Albert a right dirty look.

They pass through the next stage where the milled barley, now grist, is mixed with hot water in a huge tank called the mash tun.

                    MAIRI

        The resulting liquid is called 'wort'... which
        is drained off and then fermented... in huge
        vessels called washbacks...

She leads them through to impressively made wooden washbacks,
some 20-feet deep and some 12-feet across.

                MAIRI (CONT'D)

        These are traditionally made from Douglas
        fir... bacteria in the wood adds character to
        the mix... yeast is added and the fermentation
        begins... if you look inside you will see it all
        frothing up and bubbling away... Who has a
        sensitive nose?... I need a volunteer...

All the boys hands shoot up and they scramble over one another
to be beside her.

Rhino gets to the front beside her.

                MAIRI (CONT'D)

        [Indicating the deep frothing washback] Let
        out your breath... lean over... and take a deep
        sniff...

He does and a really sharp pain shoots up his nose and pierces
his brain.

                    RHINO

        [Grabbing his nose] Jesus Christ!

The gang has a good laugh.

                    MAIRI

        Carbon dioxide!... Very dangerous... don't do
        this at home...

Once again Robbie is last to leave. He peers into the washbacks as the others head off.

THE STILL HOUSE:
Mairi leads them into the next stage – distillation.

Harry cannot help but smile in deep satisfaction as Robbie watches him stare up in awe at the two great copper stills.

> HARRY
> [To Robbie]… like the spires on a great
> cathedral… wort into whisky… Glory be to
> Jesus…

> MAIRI
> No two stills are the same… the size, shape, and
> even the bumps on each copper still will affect
> the flavour of the whisky… it's like a big huge
> kettle…

> RHINO
> Like a big copper dick…

Rhino and Albert at the back continue their nonsense. It annoys Robbie.

> ROBBIE
> Zip it! Where's yer manners?

It shuts them up. Harry is impressed. He catches sight of Robbie, totally focussed on what Mairi is saying.

> MAIRI
> As the liquid is boiled the alcohols vaporise and
> rise up the still and over the neck… tall-necked
> stills produce a lighter spirit… stumpy stills
> allow heavier compounds to get over the neck

> resulting in a richer fuller spirit... the spirit
> cools... to become what we call 'low wines'...
> and then it is pumped [indicating] into the
> second still... and boiled up again... and it is
> here... day after day... night after night... the
> 'stillman' performs his magic. Each run has
> a beginning, middle and end... the stillman
> chooses the quality 'middle cut'... and only
> this clear precious liquid will be stored into oak
> casks for years to come...

Harry watches Robbie move to the still as the others follow Mairi out... he stares up at it, taking in every detail.

WAREHOUSE: (A TRADITIONAL DUNNAGE.)
Mairi opens several huge thick chunky locks. Mo catches Robbie's eye and smiles.

Mo automatically looks up for alarms and cameras.

Light floods into a quite beguiling space: a low stone-built earth floored 'dunnage warehouse' full of hundreds and hundreds of casks of whisky.

Mairi flicks on a few more lights and their eyes flash along rows and rows of casks stacked up more than three high.

A warehouse man comes in behind them, and he starts testing the contents of a few casks.

Mairi moves over to a cask and her hand caresses the beautiful wood in genuine appreciation.

> MAIRI (CONT'D)
> I love these casks... most were once used for
> maturing bourbon in America... but these
> bigger ones are from Spain and once held

sherry... made by hand from Spanish oak...
some crafted by a previous generation before
we were born... [tapping]...There is a subtle
reaction between the wood and the spirit...
the wood removes unwanted flavours and
adds desirable ones... but that's not all... year
after year after year these casks breathe... in
the winter they contract... in the summer
they expand... mellowing the spirit... the
transformation is miraculous...

One of the boy's lights up a cigarette, and takes a puff.

MAIRI (CONT'D)
No smoking... it's very dangerous!

YOUTH 1
[Taking a few more puffs] Just a sec hen...

Robbie loses patience and snaps it from his mouth. He spots a
sliver of light – from a long thin oblong gap – open to the fresh
air, and throws out the cigarette. Mo's eyes are drawn to the gap
too as Robbie throws the cigarette outside.

SUSAN
How long will yi keep the whisky fir?

MAIRI
10, 20, 30 even 40 years... it all depends... This
is where the mystery comes in... every cask
matures its contents slightly differently... some
can mature their contents in only five years...
in others the spirit is still immature after
twenty-five years...

MO
How much for the best one?

MAIRI

Sometimes they find a cask that takes the
breath away... a year ago they sold a single
bottle for a hundred thousand pounds...

MO

Jesus!

ALBERT

Ah could hiv bought 15 thousand bottles o'
Buckfast fir that... thirty years o' bevvy man...

MAIRI

And every year about two per cent
evaporates... disappears into thin air... gone
forever... So in a really old old cask most of the
whisky has disappeared... the Angels' Share...

ROBBIE

[To Harry] The Angels' Share... Ah like that...

The warehouse man takes a wooden mallet, a 'bung flogger', and
heads over to a barrel.

Mairi leads them out, but Robbie lingers. He is tantalised by the
mystery of it all. He too caresses a barrel and smells it. He notices
how the warehouse man whacks the barrel with the flogger to
open the wooden bung (it pops out) and drops in a dipstick, a
valinch, to extract a little of the whisky.

They all head off as Robbie's eyes dance around the dunnage
taking in every single detail.

18. TASTING ROOM AND WHISKY SHOP – LATER

All the crew are lined up along one side of a table – somehow their
trackies look even more noticeable among the fine wooden tables
and delicate glasses – as Mairi pours them all a measure of whisky.

Mo, her eyes dancing, is some distance apart, examining all the exotic bottles on the shelves as she hears Mairi's voice in the distance.

Mo comes across a whole case of miniatures, and is fascinated by the shapes and colours. There are several boxes of them waiting to go on display too.

The rest of the gang now stare in wonder at the tiny drink before them.

> MAIRI
> [As she pours out the last few drinks]... Our noses are so sensitive we can detect smells diluted to a one millionth part... our most primitive sense... right here [indicating the bridge of the nose] goes back to the time we were crawling around on our bellies as reptiles...

> RHINO
> [Nodding at Albert] Some people hivnie changed much...

> YOUTH 1
> [Holding it up in amazement] Is that a' we're gettin'?

Mairi laughs and takes it all in good spirit.

> MAIRI
> Now I want you all to smell it first... and tell me what it reminds you of?

They all sniff and are too embarrassed to say.

> MO
> Ma oul man's breath when Ah wuz a wean!

ROBBIE

Christmas cake…

Mairi is genuinely impressed. Harry smiles too.

MAIRI

Excellent! It's the fruity flavours… You have a
fine palate…

Robbie is embarrassed.

ALBERT AND RHINO

[On either side of him] Wankerrrrrr…

19. OUTSIDE DISTILLERY, BY THE VAN

Harry tries to shepherd them all back to the van. Several clamber
through the side door, two fight for the front seat, and behind,
Robbie and Mo move towards the back door.

Robbie notices that Mo's backpack is full and heavy. As she lays
it in the van by the back door he can hear the clunk of glass
against glass.

Robbie stares at Mo who looks sheepish and a bit ashamed of
herself.

MO

Ah tried ma best… [She looks at her hand
and shakes her head]… a' these pretty bright
labels… the golden colours… the shape o' the
glass… too much man… just couldnie control
masel…

Robbie zips open the top of her rucksack and grabs a handful of
miniature bottles of whisky from the top of a pile of what seems
like hundreds.

ROBBIE

[Whispering] Jesus Christ Mo… yi're a
disgrace… Harry could lose his job!

Mo nods her head in agreement.

MO

Don't even like whisky… yi want them?

ROBBIE

No Ah fucking don't… we made Harry a
promise!

Mo looks like she is genuinely ashamed of herself.

MO

Better just toss them then… eh?

Robbie hesitates for a second.

HARRY

[Shouting from the front] Come on you two…
whit's going oan?

As they get in Robbie's phone starts to ring.

He answers it as the van moves off.

Over and above the sight of the van there is the voice of someone
crying.

LEONIE VOICE OVER

Ah Robbie…

ROBBIE

What is it? Tell me!

She can't get the words out, and continues to sob.

20. SPIRES PARK, ROYSTONHILL, GLASGOW

Robbie and Leonie are in their usual secluded little spot behind the ruined church.

Leonie has a pram by her side and Luke is asleep.

Leonie is no longer sobbing, but still deeply upset by what she recalls. Robbie listens attentively.

> LEONIE
> Clancy and that guy wi the tattoo on his
> neck…

> ROBBIE
> Sniper…

> LEONIE
> They stopped me outside the house… looking
> for you… I was scared stiff…

> ROBBIE
> Did they hurt yi?

She shakes her head. She can't go on and stops for a second. Robbie's temper mounts but he tries to control himself.

> LEONIE
> That Sniper… leaned into the pram…

> ROBBIE
> Did he touch Luke?

> LEONIE
> Just tweaked his cheeks… then Clancy took
> Luke's wee hand in his and whispered 'Yi'll
> never know yer Da wee man… that's a fucking
> promise!' They burst out laughin' and went
> off…

She bursts out crying. Robbie's chest tightens.

                    LEONIE (CONT'D)
          To a baby!… It's evil! I canni stand it Robbie! I
          just want out o' here…

                    ROBBIE
          Okay sweetheart… Ah'll sort it oot…

                    LEONIE
          Sort it out!! How many times have Ah heard
          ma Da say that… all you do is make it worse
          and it goes on and on… I'm sick to ma back
          teeth!

                    ROBBIE
          Ah didn't mean that Leonie…

                    LEONIE
          I'd rather live in a cave than live like this…

She rocks the pram a little to make sure Luke is okay.

                    LEONIE (CONT'D)
          It's just a matter o' time till they find you…
          then what?

                    ROBBIE
          Ah promise Leonie… we'll find a way…

                    LEONIE
          [Looking him in the eye] How Robbie… tell
          me that?

He's ashamed he has nothing to offer and looks at his hands.

21A. ROBBIE'S BEDROOM, DOUGIE'S FLAT – EVENING

Barest of rooms with a simple mattress in the corner. There is a little lamp on the floor beside a bundle of books borrowed from the library.

Robbie, lost in thought, stares glumly at the ceiling with his hands behind his neck.

After a few moments he lets out a gentle sigh to himself.

He pulls himself up to a sitting position and takes refuge from his troubled mind by flicking through several books on whisky. He finally settles on one with lots of photographs and begins to read.

21B. STREET TO AND INTO DOUGIE'S FLAT – DAY

Mo, Rhino and Albert make their way along the street to Dougie's flat. They confront an aggressive bunch of boys by the close entry drinking cheap cider.

                    BOY 1
          Who the fuck are yous!?

A window swings open from above and Robbie peers out.

                    ROBBIE
     [Shouting down] It's okay boys… wi me.

INSIDE: the sitting room is a chaotic mess.

Dougie, Robbie's flatmate, (recognisable from the stairs earlier) half-pissed, sits on a battered old sofa in front of a TV. The image is fine, but there is no sound. Dougie is not a happy man. In massive frustration he points the controls at the telly, pressing buttons, and jabbing the air viciously as if willing the signal to jump the gap by physical force.

DOUGIE
Fuckin' volume ya bastard! Work! Work!!

His two flatmates, one a boy, the other a girl, stare meekly at the quiet image too, but say nothing.

Robbie, Albert, Rhino and Mo sit round a table in the same room. Some one hundred or so miniatures have been divided into different cluster groups.

The table too is crowded with books on whisky – opened at different pages, which Robbie has borrowed from the library.

Robbie has filled most of his notebook with tasting notes and points he wants to remember. As he noses and tastes, he scribbles down a few more notes as he tries to analyse the sample.

Many of the bottles are half empty but it is clear that the boys aren't drinking. Robbie is in the process of teaching them how to 'nose' and 'taste' the whisky. Even after they taste it, they spit the contents into a big plastic jug. It is obvious they have been at it for sometime as the plastic jug has some four inches of slops.

They are genuinely intrigued by the whole process. Rhino surveys and flicks through many of the books laid out on the table.

RHINO
[Impressed] You read a' these man?

DOUGIE
[Still jabbing with controls] Canni git the
fucker oot the library these days… the library!!
[Hurling the controls – it explodes against the
wall] Shite!

ROBBIE
[Quietly to mates at table] Dae yi blame me?

ALBERT

[Pouring] Right guess this one…

They share two white wine glasses between the group. Robbie noses it carefully as the boys watch.

Dougie's eyes flick between TV screen, and then the boys.

DOUGIE

Been daein that a' fucking week!! Sniff sniff sniff… are yi gonni gi me a drink or no?

Robbie doesn't even acknowledge him. Dougie turns back to the silent image again.

ROBBIE

Look at the colour… pale gold… [nosing only] then yi 'nose it'…

DOUGIE

'Nose it'… pervert!

ROBBIE

Nose… [nosing again]… heavy sweet and peaty… there's a whiff o' sea breeze man… it's an island malt for cert…

He passes it to Albert who noses too as Robbie writes down his notes. The boys pass the two glasses round, nosing the glasses.

ALBERT

[Doubtful] Sea breeze… a' we need noo is the rainbow…

RHINO

[Nose] Know whit yi mean… it is salty…

MO

But it's sweet tae…

ALBERT

Bullshit… a' the same tae me…

MO

[Holding up the glass for him] Can yi no smell the peat?

DOUGIE

What the fuck is peat?

RHINO

It comes fae the ground… they dig it up…

DOUGIE

And then throw it in a drink! Nae wonder it tastes shite…

Albert spits it out into the jug slops and his face contorts.

ALBERT

He's right…

ROBBIE

Gi' yersel time… Ah wuz the same… big Harry has been teachin' me… right… 'taste'…

Robbie takes the glass and adds in a little water… and then drinks. He rolls it round his mouth slowly and deliberately and then spits it out into the jug.

ROBBIE (CONT'D)

Peaty… a bit spicy… wi' a hint of nut and maybe… lemon… but Ah'm no sure…

The others do the same as Albert views it all like a doubting Thomas. At his turn, Albert really makes a meal of it, spitting out more than just whisky into the jug; and then one more revolting addition just for good measure.

MO

Nutty… fuck's sake… aye!! Ah get yi… where's
that come fae?

ROBBIE

The casks… maybe a short fermentation…
American oak gives vanilla and coconut
flavours… even chocolate…

ALBERT

That's it! [Incredulous, banging the table] Sea
breeze, nutty, and noo coconut! Yi're a' setting
me up! Think Ah'm stupid?!

MO

Aye. Dumb as fuck… just listen Albert…

RHINO

[Nosing]… Canni believe we're drinkin' and
no gettin's wasted man…

DOUGIE

[Still transfixed by the quiet telly] Neither can
Ah! Need a fucking drink!

ALBERT

[To Robbie, and hiding the bottle in his fist]
Right… what is it?

ROBBIE

Ah'd say a Talisker…

Albert smiles and shakes his head, as he turns the miniature round.

ROBBIE (CONT'D)

[Shaking his head]… A Caol Ila. Baith island
whiskies…

ALBERT

Bullshiter!

Rhino, still with a book, mouths the words to himself…

RHINO

Are these guys serious… [now reading] 'Smells
detonate softly in our memory like poignant
land mines hidden under the weedy mass of
years…'

Dougie lets out a roaring corker of an elongated fart that nearly
blows a hole in the settee.

Yells of disgust.

RHINO (CONT'D)

Fuckin' skunk!

DOUGIE

Skunkie needs a drink!

Dougie stands up and marches over to the table. He takes one look
at them and then grabs the plastic jug full of slops and downs it
all in a oner, gulp after gulp.

He wipes his lips.

DOUGIE (CONT'D)

Peaty, but a bit lumpy.

The boys wet themselves laughing.

22. SNOOKER HALL – DAY

The white ball smacks powerfully against a new frame of red balls
which scatter noisily around the table.

Robbie and Mo play snooker against Rhino and Albert. They are at the end table – one of around six, by the far end of the hall.

Albert takes ages to line up a shot as Rhino waits impatiently. Albert misses by a mile, as Rhino's face drops.

ALBERT
Light in here is shite by the way…

RHINO
Ah'd be better aff playin' wi Stevie Wonder…

Mo is terrific and pots a long ball. Robbie punches the air and there is a grin between them.

Mo catches the door swing open just a little and then close. Her face darkens. But it goes all quiet again.

As Robbie leans in to take a shot, the door opens a little more. Mo is wary and keeps her eye on it. A young lad enters and moves towards another table. She relaxes.

A shot now by Rhino.

Suddenly the door bursts open. Clancy, Sniper and three mates rush towards them screaming.

VOICES
Fucking get him!

MO
[Screaming] Run Robbie… Run!

Mo blocks the narrow space between the tables and bravely swings her cue wildly as she screams at them. Her frenzied antics delay them for a few moments and gives Robbie a few seconds to run along the side of the hall and crash through an emergency door.

The alarm goes off. Chaos. Robbie sprints down the stairs and they give chase.

STREET: Robbie runs for his life pursued by Clancy and co still armed with snooker cues.

Robbie runs between bodies on the pavement. A women screams in fright.

Robbie trips and scrambles up again.

The boys gain on him. Clancy is really fast.

Robbie runs out onto the road and dangerously weaves between traffic. Horns and screeching of brakes as the gang follows.

By the side of the road again; they all pant from the exertion as Clancy and Sniper gradually close on him.

Robbie turns to face them. Just 20 yards between them.

ROBBIE

 Fuck you!

All are gasping for breath. The others catch up. Clancy pulls a knife from his jacket.

Sniper pulls a knife from his jacket too, and it flicks open. They move towards him as Robbie desperately looks around him.

Deafening screeching of brakes by Robbie. A powerful Mercedes is right beside him.

Robbie can't believe his eyes as he confronts Leonie's father Matt in the driver's seat.

ROBBIE (CONT'D)

 Ah shit…

MATT

Thought it wuz fuckin' you! Get in!

He just manages to scramble in before the boys get to him. A snooker cue smashes against the windscreen as the car speeds off.

23. ROAD TO AND OUTSIDE DOUGIE'S FLAT

FROM OUTSIDE THE CAR: The Merc speeds along main arteries, then down a busy road before turning off into increasingly ugly open spaces and exposed gable ends of abandoned council houses towards Dougie's flat where Robbie still stays.

INSIDE: They drive in complete silence.

At last Matt pulls up at speed outside Dougie's flat. Some of the same boys who were drinking at the close entry when Mo, Rhino and Albert arrived are there again, drinking, and killing time.

Sudden hush inside the car as Matt cuts the engine.

ROBBIE

Ta.

Matt glances round the place and focusses in on the boys drinking at the close.

MATT

Nice place to bring up a wean eh?

ROBBIE

Why can't yi give me a chance… that's all
Ah'm askin'… just one mair chance…

MATT

Did that with Leonie's sister… gave the prick
just one mair chance… yi know how that
ended up don't yi?

ROBBIE

Ah'll look after Leonie... Ah'm gonnie be a
good Da...

Matt turns glances at him. Not without understanding.

MATT

[Quietly] You don't get it dae yi?... Too late
fir you... even if yi want tae change... they
won't let yi... think yi can reason wi the
likes o' Clancy? Call it quits?! [Pause]... Ah
see cunts like you every day in the bar...
kiddin' themselves on... [Pause, with genuine
conviction] Ah'm trying tae dae the best thing
for Leonie and the baby... think long term...
she's young... she'll learn...

Silence.

MATT (CONT'D)

Yir only chance is ootside Glasgow... Ah'll
give yi five grand tae head tae London...
Five! On your own. New start. Look at yersel
Robbie... [he feels humiliated] What can you
offer ma daughter?

He gives him a chance to answer. Silence.

MATT (CONT'D)

Look at this shithole... you, wi yer chibbed
face, done time... yi'll never git work... even
the army won't touch yi wi a bargepole... can
you no see Leonie and Vincent are better aff
without yi...

Pause, confusion, then shock, on Robbie's face.

ROBBIE

Vincent?

MATT

Aye, 'Vincent'... Leonie's son, my grandchild...
Vincent.

Robbie stares at him.

ROBBIE

[Holding his eye] My son's name is Luke.

Matt's face changes as he stares ahead.

He turns to look at a defiant Robbie.

MATT

Out! Yi won't be lucky every day.

Robbie gets out. The Merc's wheels spin viciously as the car tears
off.

Desolate, Robbie heads for the close to the flat.

BOY 1

[Holding out a 3-litre bottle] Fancy a wee
sensation Robbie boy...

He walks through them without saying a word.

24. COMMUNITY SERVICE – SIGHTHILL CEMETERY – DAY

Victorian section of a cemetery on a hill with some spectacular
views over the city.

The majority of the gravestones are lopsided and covered in moss.
Many of the names of the deceased are faded beyond recognition.

Robbie, Mo, Albert, Rhino, Susan, PC, and perhaps three others, with Harry supervising, are in the process of cleaning up the gravestones with high pressure hoses, or trying to push them up into their proper position.

Quiet dignified sense of decorum as they perform their tasks.

Albert passes by Rhino. The latter is bent over, working on a flat gravestone. Albert can't resist the temptation and gives him a quick 'skoosh' with the hose. Rhino jumps out of his skin.

> RHINO
> [Pissed off] Fuckin' soaking pants ya prick!

> ALBERT
> Consecrated ground man… some respect.

> SUSAN
> Bad karma… tell him Harry…

> RHINO
> Soggy arse, in a graveyard, wi' a dunce…

> PC
> That's the life…

> HARRY
> Cool it Albert… it's no the place…

Albert, experimenting, skooshes his own arse with the hose.

> ALBERT
> No that bad… quite fresh.

Several of the others laugh at his nonsense.

Harry can see that Robbie is down, and doesn't join in the banter with the others. Harry approaches him to give him a hand as Robbie tries to straighten up a gravestone.

HARRY

What's up?

ROBBIE

Nuthin…

HARRY

Are Leonie and Luke okay?

ROBBIE

Fine… everything's just fucking perfect.

Robbie and Harry push the gravestone into position and then Robbie uses a spade to fill the soil in on one side to give it more support.

He looks pissed off and in a black mood.

HARRY

Ah'm going tae Edinburgh at the weekend… a
whisky show… yi want to come?

It raises Robbie's spirits slightly. Albert and co overhear, and tune in straightaway.

ROBBIE

Skint man…

HARRY

Ah'll get yer ticket… come on…

ALBERT AND RHINO

Can Ah come? Me tae?

MO

We've never been tae Edinburgh… Ah'll dae
the sandwiches…

Harry looks round at their expectant faces covered in grime.

HARRY

Ah Jaysus…

25. WAVERLEY TRAIN STATION, THEN PRINCES STREET, EDINBURGH

CONCOURSE: Robbie, Mo, Albert and Rhino, dressed in their usual trackies, accompanied by Harry – smartly dressed, walk up to the barriers and pass on through. The trains are visible behind them.

They walk up a steep set of steps that leads on to the glory of Princes Street. Harry notices them all soaking it in.

Albert stops dead as he spots something.

ALBERT

What the fuck is that?

It takes some figuring out what he means.

ALBERT (CONT'D)

[Pointing] That!

RHINO

It's the castle ya moron… Edinburgh Castle.

ALBERT

What did they pit it way up there fir?

26. ENTRANCE TO LUXURY EDINBURGH HOTEL – DAY

Harry, walking in front, leads them to the entrance of a grand hotel. He notices that they are behind. He turns to look at them, and can see they are hesitant about entering.

HARRY

Come on… what's up?

They still look nervous and out of their depth.

ROBBIE

Are you sure they'll let us in?

Harry beckons them in.

Albert, like a child, stares up at the height of the ceilings and enormous chandeliers.

Mo's eyes clock the foreign tourists in amazement as Harry asks the receptionist where the event is being held.

Robbie stares at two very sophisticated young women who glide down the stairs in expensive clothing.

He shuffles in his embarrassment.

INSIDE AN ELEGANT WOODEN PANELLED ROOM: WHISKY SHOW:

RORY McALLISTER, larger than life, charismatic, engaging, and 'Grand Master of the Quaich' (an honourary title in the whisky industry) leads a blind tasting.

The audience is a good mix of foreign and Scottish malt whisky enthusiasts.

Rory really gives a show. He talks with great enthusiasm, knowledge, but he does not show-off or try to embarrass his volunteers.

In the front row, a memorable character, THADDEUS, in his forties, watches carefully.

He is casually dressed, but with the most expensive clothes. He has intelligent eyes and misses nothing. (Cf appendix 2 - page 173.)

A suited ASSISTANT announces the star presenter.

ASSISTANT

Ladies and Gentlemen… as you know this is
a charity event and before we move on to the
auction… may I present to you The Grand
Master of the Quaich… Mr Rory McAllister…

Enthusiastic applause as Rory takes centre position.

RORY

Thank you… Now I need four volunteers for
a blind tasting… this is all just a bit of fun…
You Sir…What's your name and where are you
from?

VOLUNTEER 1

[Standing up and coming forward] Garrett…
from Oakland, California…

RORY

You sir…

VOLUNTEER 2

Satoshi from Tokyo…

RORY

[Spotting Robbie] Now how about one of you
young lads… [they all visibly shrink into their
shells] Yes, you at the end… Come on!… Just
some mischief, I'm not the dentist… Come on!

Robbie is even more embarrassed by everyone now looking at
him. Rhino and Mo try to push him up as Robbie tells them
under his breath to fuck off.

HARRY

Come on Robbie… Ah'll come up with yi…

Harry grabs his arm and pulls him up as the crowd give encouragement by clapping.

                    RORY
        What's your name and where are you from?

                    ROBBIE
        Robbie... fae Carntyne...

Albert, Mo and Rhino are pissing themselves at Robbie's discomfort. He looks totally incongruous in his trackies, beside all the suits. His eyes dart from the crowd to his shoes, and he doesn't know what to do with his hands.

But he fascinates Thaddeus.

                    HARRY
        Harry... from Glasgow...

Rory's assistant pours out the drinks from a bottle which has the label covered into nosing glasses.

                    RORY
        [Studying the colour, watching the tears
        down the glass] Some people have a great ear
        for music... some have wonderful eye-to-
        hand coordination and become world class
        sportsmen... and some people are born with an
        incredibly sensitive palate...

Thaddeus studies Robbie. Despite him looking like a fish out of water, Thaddeus notices how he holds the glass, noses the whisky and holds it up to the light to examine the tears running down the side.

                    RORY (CONT'D)
        [Nosing] Lovely lovely... rich... I'd say
        medium sweet... flowery... with a note of

herbs… just a touch of smoke… a wet dog on
a rainy day…

He encourages the others to join in. They taste a little and Rory
encourages them to speak.

> AMERICN TOURIST
> Medium bodied… firm… malty with a touch
> of peat… very good…

> JAPANESE TOURIST
> I detect honey and fruity notes…

> HARRY
> Aye… a bit of honey and spice Ah think…

> RORY
> Very good… excellent… I'd agree with that…
> Robbie… and by the way… great to see a
> young man in here with us… curiosity beyond
> vodka and coke always cheers me up… What
> do you think?

Robbie feels overwhelmed with the attention, shrugs his shoulders,
and looks to the ground. Albert and co are grinning away.

> RORY (CONT'D)
> Well… moment of truth… any guesses?

> AMERICAN TOURIST
> I'd guess it's a Speyside… but I really don't
> know…

> JAPANESE TOURIST
> I guess an Aberfeldy…

> RORY
> Good… Harry?

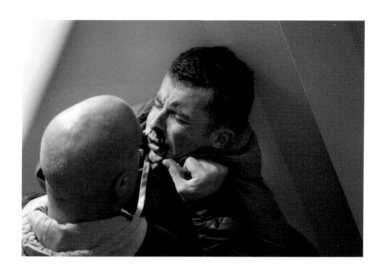

HARRY

Definitely a Speyside... maybe an Aberlour?

Thaddeus notices Robbie shaking his head ever so slightly, and leaning into Harry.

RORY

[Enthusiastic] Very interesting choice... you are
in the right cluster... Robbie... any ideas?

He looks up at the crowd and Albert giving him the wanker's sign from the back of the room. He just shakes his head.

RORY (CONT'D)

Go on have a guess.

Robbie suddenly stares out at the audience, just as he did from the dock. He doesn't hide from eye contact. The silence makes them all the more attentive.

ROBBIE

No sure... between a Glenfarclas and a
Cragganmore...

RORY

I'll be damned!... Thought the same... which
one Robbie?

He hesitates.

ROBBIE

Glenfarclas...

RORY

Okay... I'll go for the Cragganmore...

Rory's assistant takes the cover off the bottle.

RORY (CONT'D)
A Cragganmore!

There is enthusiastic response from the audience, and Rory, pointing at Robbie, applauds him, as Harry smiles too in satisfaction at his close call.

Thaddeus watches Robbie take his seat and continues to scrutinise him.

JAPANESE TOURIST
Sure you are sick of this question Sir... but what is the best whisky you have ever tasted?

Rory chuckles.

RORY
I've been writing about whisky for over 35 years... and last night... just last night... I returned from... [pause] Paradise! I was asked to write up tasting notes for... [Pause, leaving it blank – laughter, he shakes his head]... it was the best dram... ever made by human hand... ever... it literally is one in a billion!

A ripple of excitement runs through the room of enthusiasts.

VOICES
You have to tell us! What was it?! Come on Rory!!

RORY
It was a freak discovery... we think it must have been a swap of casks between two managers in different distilleries whose children married each other in the same year... [pause] 1960... a strange quirk of fate...

Thaddeus is immediately alert.

> RORY (CONT'D)
> The distillery where it was made doesn't exist
> any more [Thaddeus grins and he nods to
> himself as Rory delights in their attention]…
> it has been over 50 years in a totally unique
> sherry cask in a traditional dunnage… after so
> many years they estimate there might only be
> enough for a half dozen bottles at the most…
> believe me… you will read about this in the
> news… it will go to public auction in the next
> two weeks… the tragedy is it will never see the
> light of day again… it will go to the bunker of
> some billionaire in China or Russia… but it
> was sublime… the nearest a man can get to the
> beatific vision!

> VOICE
> How much is worth?

Mo's eyes are flashing.

> RORY
> Priceless… I can hardly imagine…

> MANY VOICES
> Which distillery Rory?… You have to tell us!?
> Is it a Speyside? Just a hint Rory…

> RORY
> [Laughing, and trying to calm them down]
> Okay… okay okay… just among us…
> [pause]… It is situated somewhere between…
> Hadrian's Wall… and the Shetlands…

More laughter and then applause.

Outside the hall, by a bookstand on whisky. Robbie flicks through the books.

Thaddeus approaches.

> THADDEUS
>
> Well done.

Robbie just looks at him.

> THADDEUS (CONT'D)
>
> Surprised them didn't you?

Again, Robbie just holds his eye.

> THADDEUS (CONT'D)
>
> Never judge a book by its cover eh?

Thaddeus takes a little sampling bottle from his pocket and hands it to Robbie.

> THADDEUS (CONT'D)
>
> What's that?

Robbie opens it and smells it.

> ROBBIE
>
> Easy...

Thaddeus can tell by his eye he knows.

> THADDEUS
>
> [Nodding at his cheek] Where did you pick up that... prison or a bar?

> ROBBIE
>
> Why... fuckin' like one?

> THADDEUS
>
> Easy Robbie… some of my best friends are
> inside…

A moment between them.

> ROBBIE
>
> Who are you?

Thaddeus hands him his business card.

> THADDEUS
>
> Thaddeus… a simple collector…

He walks off to catch Rory, the Grand Master.

> RORY
>
> Ah Thaddeus…

They shake hands. Robbie pays close attention.

> THADDEUS
>
> It's a Malt Mill isn't?

Robbie makes a mental note of the name.

> RORY
>
> You old bloodhound… that's what brings you
> here… who have you been speaking to?

> THADDEUS
>
> Word travels fast. I'm stunned.

Robbie studies them; Rory deflects further questions with laughter
and says his goodbyes as he picks up his briefcase from a table and
leaves the room.

RECEPTION TO HOTEL: Mo watches Rory head for the
reception and follows from a distance. Rory lays the briefcase

down as he fills out a form at the reception. Half way through doing so, GARRETT, volunteer tourist from Arizona, moves over to him. Rory turns to him to shake hands as the conversation between them continues.

Rory has his back to the briefcase.

Mo's eyes are flashing as she moves at speed to the desk.

27. WAVERLEY TRAIN STATION, EDINBURGH – DAY

Harry, Rhino, Albert, Mo and Robbie wait on a busy platform for the Glasgow train.

HARRY
Any o' yis want a juice?

Harry heads into a little shop/cafeteria just beside the platform and is followed in by Rhino and Albert.

Mo spots her chance and moves in close to Robbie. He notices her excitement.

MO
It was just a hunch… Ah followed him tae the reception…

ROBBIE
What are yi talking aboot?

MO
The Grand Master! At the hotel… he left his briefcase doon… [pulling out a file in a plastic cover from under her jumper] Nicked this fae inside… [pause] Ah know the distillery… Ah know which cask!

ROBBIE
Are yi mad?

MO

Oor big chance Robbie…

ROBBIE

If Ah get caught Ah'll dae five years… at least.

MO

Who'd ever suspect scruffs like us?

They both glance round quickly and can see Harry pay for the drinks through the windows.

ROBBIE

Ah've promised Leonie… Nae mair shite from me!… Mo, how long hiv Ah known yi?

MO

Since primary school…

ROBBIE

And yi git caught every time… just stop it! Fuck's sake!

She stuffs the plastic file up her jumper just as Harry brings them a juice.

28. TENEMENT FLAT, PARTICK, WEST END OF GLASGOW

Robbie, again carrying Luke in a Wilkinet, and Leonie walk down a very pleasant sandstoned street full of red tenement flats.

They stop at another tasteful close. It has a nice little green space before it, even some flowers that have been carefully attended.

Leonie and Robbie stop, and stare up in amazement at the facade.

LEONIE

It's gorgeous…

ROBBIE

Sure yi hiv the right address Leonie?

LEONIE

Positive…

He doesn't follow Leonie to the close. He is hesitant and fearful.

ROBBIE

Maybe Ah should wait ootside… don't want
tae fuck it a' up.

LEONIE

She knows all about yi Robbie… she's ma
aunt's best pal… come on.

He reluctantly follows.

INSIDE THE FLAT: it is a simple two-bedroom flat, but somehow
elegant.

A bright woman, GRACE, in her early thirties shows them round
the kitchen. Leonie beams, while Robbie still looks distrustful.

GRACE

It's a new boiler so you'll have no problems…
it's really cosy… it's on a timer so just change it
to suit yourselves… come on… show you the
bedrooms…

Robbie lingers behind and he can hear the two of them chat. His
eyes scan everything, and he's amazed at how comfortable it all is.

He catches up with them in the bedrooms.

LEONIE

Look Robbie… this'll be Luke's room…

Robbie nods and looks around. It looks lovely, but he doesn't say anything.

LEONIE (CONT'D)
[To Grace] He's actually quite shy…

GRACE
I'll show you the other room…

They walk into the second bedroom.

LEONIE
It's beautiful! Robbie… what do you think?

Grace smiles. Robbie still looks withdrawn.

ROBBIE
You don't mind if Ah move in wi Leonie?

GRACE
You are together aren't yi?

ROBBIE
And her Da will no find oot?

GRACE
It's okay Robbie… I know Leonie's aunt from way back… did nursing together… like sisters.

ROBBIE
Why are yi daein' this fir us?

Leonie is stunned by the question, but Grace appreciates his directness.

GRACE
Someone gave me a chance once… changed my life. Sounds like you two deserve a bit of luck… and I'm only away in London for three months anyway.

Robbie stares at her for a moment.

> ROBBIE
> Thank you Grace.

He walks out towards the kitchen as the two women look at each other.

> LEONIE
> [Whispering] He just canni believe it…

Robbie stares out the back window onto a delightful shared back garden with clothes lines dangling. He leans his head on the window and looks almost overcome.

29. STREET OUTSIDE THE FLAT

The walk out of the close to Grace's car. As Leonie gets into the back seat Robbie hands over the baby.

> GRACE
> I can drop you off in the city centre… is that okay?

> LEONIE
> That's fantastic… thanks for everything Grace… [really touched] you'll never know what this means to us… never.

Robbie nods too.

> GRACE
> Away yi go…

Just as Robbie is about to jump in too he notices a body dart behind a hedge two closes up. His face changes, but he tries to hide it from Leonie.

ROBBIE

Leonie... you go... Ah'll catch yi later...
thanks Grace.

LEONIE

What's up?

ROBBIE

Dae yi mind if Ah just walk aroon on ma
own... just to see whit the area feels like... it's
still a bit o' a shock...

She smiles.

LEONIE

Okay... phone me.

The car takes off.

Once it is around the corner Robbie walks at speed to the next
close. He peers round the corner of the hedge. He stares at Sniper
(distinctive tattoo up round his neck) trying to find some shade
by the close entrance as he texts someone. He sends the text and
looks up a split second before Robbie collides with him at speed
knocking him flat on his back onto the steps.

Robbie has him tight by the collar of his jacket and his knuckles
dig deep into his throat. Robbie is white with fury and squeezes
him tighter, half throttling him.

ROBBIE

What the fuck are you doing here?

SNIPER

Nuthin...

ROBBIE

Fuckin' followed me!

SNIPER

Visitin' a mate man…

Robbie catches him trying to grasp something from his jacket pocket. Robbie clips him a good one to the chin with his elbow and grasps his hand which now has a flick knife open. Robbie smashes his hand against the step and the knife drops. Robbie grasps it, and sticks it to his throat – Sniper stretches his head back against the blade which now painfully jabs his skin.

Robbie has a rage to him that terrifies Sniper.

ROBBIE

Dae yi no fuckin' understand ya prick!!

Robbie grabs his hair with the other hand and yanks his head back, exposing his throat even more.

ROBBIE (CONT'D)

Ah want fuckin' peace! Want tae look after ma boy! Never want to see you or Clancy again! Dae yi fuckin' get it?!! [screaming at him] Ah want out! Nae mair [jabbing, increasing the pressure till he whimpers] shite!! Ah want a fuckin' life!!

He tries to calm himself, and takes a couple of deep breaths.

ROBBIE (CONT'D)

[Whispering] Now tell me the truth… or yi'll get it. [Pause] Did yi follow me?

Sniper nods.

ROBBIE (CONT'D)

How?

                                   SNIPER

Ma motorbike… across the road… Clancy told
me to follow yi…

                                   ROBBIE

Hiv yi told him yet?

                                   SNIPER

No… Ah promise… Ah'll never tell him…

                                   ROBBIE

Who did yi text?

                                   SNIPER

Just ma mate…

                                   ROBBIE

Gi' me yer phone… if yi're lying…

                                   SNIPER

Ah'm sorry man… please Robbie… yi know
whit he's like… Ah had to tell him… Ah had
tae man…

                                   ROBBIE

He knows the address? [Only terror on his
face] Fuckin' tell me!

Sniper, petrified, nods his head.

The look in Robbie's eye terrifies him even more.

                                   SNIPER

Please Robbie… Clancy made me…

                                   ROBBIE

Where's that cunt living?

Robbie increases the pressure till it just about breaks the skin.

SNIPER

Still wi his brother… above the bar… you
know the one.

Robbie just stares at him. He lifts the knife from his throat and
strokes the tip of the blade along one cheek and then the other
leaving the slightest of marks, as a long fingernail might do.

ROBBIE

Yi just fucked up our whole life…

He glances around him. No one.

ROBBIE (CONT'D)

[Quiet] Ah feel nuthin… [meaning it] Ah could
dae yi right noo…

The knife weaves in front of his throat.

For one second it really looks like he might do it.

Sniper begins to sob.

He pounds the knife down – the handle of the blade grazing his
ear and smashing against the step.

Robbie stands up and walks off. He passes by a motorbike. On
impulse he boots it over and it crashes down.

He stabs and rips at the tyre; air pumps out as rubber is sliced into
jagged ribbons. He shocks himself at his own fury.

Another motorbike screeches to a halt 30 yards from him.

SNIPER

Wrang bike ya prick!… Should hiv taken yir
chance!

He gives him the middle finger and accelerates off.

30. BAR, GLASGOW – EVENING

Robbie, in a corner of a busy working men's bar, watches Harry wait for his order and joke with the regulars. He is popular and at ease.

Harry approaches him with two whiskies and a grin on his face.

HARRY
This'll cheer yi up. Right... what is it?

Robbie can barely raise the energy to answer, and shakes his head.

HARRY (CONT'D)
Come on...

Robbie copies Harry, adds a little water, and then tastes. He can't bear to disappoint him.

ROBBIE
[Resigned] 'Glen of Tranquility'... Sixteen Men of Tain... founded 1849... [looking into the glass] Glenmorangie...

HARRY
[Genuinely impressed] Yi'r way ahead o' me...

ROBBIE
Got fuck all else tae dae... kept me sane.

Harry stares at Robbie.

HARRY
So whit's up?

Long silence.

ROBBIE

Ah'm gonni fucking explode Harry... can
smell it... Ah'm scared Ah'm gonni hurt
someone... comin' at me like a train... and Ah
just canni seem tae move...

HARRY

Somethin' happen?

ROBBIE

Ah was that close [indicating] tae takin'
someone oot... that close!... Really scared
masel... Leonie's Da was right... been kiddin'
masel on... once yer in the shit yi just canni
bail oot... they just won't let yi...

HARRY

Got tae keep oot of their way...

Robbie hands Harry his mobile, and he reads the text.

HARRY (CONT'D)

'Dead meat...tick tock tick tock...' [Shaking
his head]... That boy Clancy?

ROBBIE

It's me or him... toss up between us... feel like
a fuckin' rat in a corner...

A moment between them.

ROBBIE (CONT'D)

Ah'm gonni fuck off tae London.

Harry is stunned.

ROBBIE (CONT'D)

Psychobaws offered me five grand...

HARRY

[Confused] Leonie's Da... he's gonni help yis?

He stares at Robbie for a moment. The penny drops.

HARRY (CONT'D)

No way! Buyin' yi aff! Ah don't believe it...
naw... yi're gonni leave Leonie and Luke!

ROBBIE

Ah canni even git an interview fir a part-time
cleaning job... a lollipop man!... Even the
army knocked me back. Ah'll never work if Ah
stay... if Ah leave... bring Leonie tae a fuckin'
hameless unit in Birmingham? Better where
she is.

HARRY

If yi leave them now... time passes, things
change... might never get them back... there
must be something else Robbie... must be!

Harry sips his whisky. Robbie picks up his and sips too. He stares
down at his half-empty glass for a few moments.

ROBBIE

Have you ever tasted a Malt Mill?

HARRY

A Malt Mill! In ma dreams... it's 'the' Holy
Grail.

A moment between them.

ROBBIE

Can you lend me five hundred quid?

Harry nearly chokes on his whisky.

HARRY

Five hundred quid! Are you joking?

He looks up at Robbie who stares at him in deadly seriousness.

HARRY (CONT'D)

Will Ah git it back?

ROBBIE

Don't know.

HARRY

Yi're no gonni gamble wi it… are yi?

ROBBIE

Yeah… the biggest gamble o' ma life.

31. DOUGIE'S FLAT – DAY

Robbie flips over a page of the document, and his eyes flash. Mo, Rhino, and Albert sit round the table alongside him.

Robbie flicks over a few more pages.

ROBBIE

His tasting notes… [eyes flashing over the notes]… fucking hell… [reading] 'This is without doubt a genuine Malt Mill… I have checked the provenance in exhaustive detail, and every step makes sense… Almost certainly it is the only cask left in existence, and since there are only three bottles left in the world, and two of these are suspected fakes, every serious collector in the world would pay a fortune… since there may only be enough for some half dozen bottles it is likely that the sale could raise in excess of one million pounds…'

RHINO

A million smackeronies!

Silence. The gang look at each other. Mo holds up her hand.

MO

Ma hand's tremblin'… ma body's shakin'… ma
guts are tinglin'…

ALBERT

If yi were a man… Yi'd hiv a hard-on…

Albert and Rhino glance at each other.

Robbie's eyes greedily scan the notes. He mouths the words to
himself as the boys watch.

He can hardly control his excitement, and has to jump up and
walk over to the window.

ALBERT (CONT'D)

What is it?

ROBBIE

They'll dae the auction where the cask is…
way up north by the Dornoch Firth… A world
event… 'the genuine Scottish experience'…
dae a' that Highland shit that has the yanks
comin' in their pants… invite the richest
collectors… on the night before the auction
they'll hiv a 'tasting' with the Grand Master…
followed by a ceilidh at the local hotel…

ALBERT

What the fuck is a 'Firth'? [in response to their
confusion] Dornoch Firth! Probably need
huskies… maybe even a boat…depending what
it is…

MO

And even if we find it... how would we git
away with it?... Probably like fucking Alcatraz
man...

RHINO

And even if we got it... whose's gonni take it
fae scruffs like us?! It's the equivalent o' hivin
Mona Lisa in yer bedroom!

ALBERT

Mona who?

RHINO

Mona! Lisa!!

ALBERT

Just askin'... fuck's sake...

ROBBIE

We'd hiv to find a collector... who wanted it...
for just hivin' it... because he 'knows' and it's
'his'... like these rich fuckers wi stolen Picassos'
in their basement...

MO

Way above oor league man...

RHINO

Impossible... no way... we'll git caught. We're
a' just dreamin... forget it man...

ALBERT

[Enjoying the words] 'Dornoch Firth'... bet it's
a' misty and full o' bagpipes man...

Robbie's mind is racing. He stares out the window for a few moments and then down at Dougie's cans and miscellaneous bottles – including the obligatory Irn-Bru bottle. (A Scottish soft drink famed for helping hangovers. It has an orange-like colour inside the bottle.)

ROBBIE

[Silence as they look at him, puzzled] When Ah was in remand Ah met this oul lag... smart as fuck... always readin'... he told me aboot an oul tale... An Arab smuggler used to take his donkey across the border every day wi bags loaded wi straw... [now they are mesmerized]... he admitted he was a smuggler... the guards searched him, his donkey, and the bags every single day but could never find anythin'... sometimes they even burnt the straw... still he got richer and richer and richer... it drove them mad fir years... Eventually he retired and moved off... one of the guards found him as an old man... and said... 'You can tell us now... what were you smuggling?' The old man smiled and said 'Donkeys'.

The boys look at each other. Silence as it sinks in.

ALBERT

How in the name of fuck can we git a donkey way up there...

Robbie, Rhino and Mo shake their heads. Robbie looks at the cans and bottles surrounding his spot. Something catches Robbie's attention.

He picks up the bottle of Irn-Bru – half consumed, and holds it up to the light. It's not perfect, but with a little imagination, it could almost pass for whisky. They look at each other.

RHINO

Anyway… look at us… we'd stick oot like sare thumbs up there… might as well hiv criminals tattooed on our heids! If we got trackies on we're neds… if we wear suits… looks like we're gonni tae court…

MO

That's true…[to Robbie]… especially you…

Silence.

ALBERT

Kilts… kilts. Naebody bothers anybody wearing a kilt… we'll look friendly wee cunts up the Highlands man… whisky trainspotters… know whit Ah mean?

The others look at each other, thinking, and deeply impressed.

ROBBIE

[Pointing at him] Albert… Albert Einstein!!

It doesn't register with him.

RHINO

Never mind… a friend o' Mona's.

Robbie throws down £500 on the table which amazes them.

ROBBIE

For kilts… a tent… and three days sandwiches.

ALBERT

Dornoch Firth!

32. HITCH-HIKING TRIP

Dual carriageway, with city scape behind: over and above the song from the Proclaimers 'I'm Gonna Be (500 Miles)' (up beat, populist, and exploding with optimism) lorries, buses and other vehicles flash past in a blur.

In a gap between the traffic, four strange figures come into focus; Robbie, Rhino, and Albert, wearing kilts, and Mo, with tartan trousers, heavy boots, and maybe a cheeky tartan cap – all carrying rucksacks, stand hitching a lift.

They look like they have been there for some time and not in the best of form. Robbie glances at his watch, as Mo gives a passing vehicle the fingers at it blows its horn but doesn't stop.

Out of the blue a 12-seater minivan pulls to a halt and swerves in.

They screech with delight and run to the vehicle and scramble in.

INSIDE: their faces stare in awe as they confront a vehicle full of six smiling nuns in full penguin gear.

ALBERT
Fuck me… the Sound o' Music!

Robbie elbows him in the stomach.

ROBBIE
Sorry Sisters… a Protestant.

LATER: in stunning countryside, perhaps by a loch, a battered and muddied four-wheel drive Jeep carrying a trailer full of enormous pigs drops the gang off by another junction.

As the Jeep pulls off, the kids are laughing their heads off as Albert and Mo hold their noses. They mess around the empty countryside like lost lambs, intoxicated by the adventure.

They are dropped off by another vehicle at a scenic viewing point filled with several cars.

Stunning weather, and outrageously beautiful views.

The gang's eyes are on the scenery, but not for long. Three young French students (female) ask to have their photographs taken with them. A French boy approaches Mo, who looks deadly embarrassed.

One pose after another as they spin their yarns.

The song ends.

> RHINO
> [To the prettiest French girl]... Ma great great great great great grandfather... was in the battle o' Glencoe... a Highland chief...

> GIRL
> What was his name?

> RHINO
> Hamish McTavish... that's why Ah wear the McTavish tartan wi such pride to this day...

She looks him up and down, quite impressed.

> GIRL
> Is that why you wear it back to front?

The others laugh as Rhino looks down at his kilt.

> GIRL (CONT'D)
> But the big question is... what is underneath?

> RHINO
> That's where Ah store ma bagpipes darlin'...

GIRL

Are they back to front as well?

She walks off with an impish grin.

The boys, eyes shining, stare after them as they wave goodbye.

33. COUNTRY ROAD, BY A DISTILLERY, DORNOCH FIRTH

Brow of a hill. The narrow country road looks out over stunning countryside.

First Robbie, with his shirt off, and then Rhino, with shirt over his shoulder, (both translucent white), gradually come over the brow, followed by Mo. They are obviously not used to the outdoor life, and have struggled with Mother Nature. As they get to the brow of the hill, sweating and panting after their long walk, they look down on Albert 60 yards below them. He walks with a strange waddle.

ROBBIE

[Shouting at him] Whit's wrong wi yi... hurry up!

Albert shouts back through cupped hands.

ALBERT

This sporran keeps bouncing on ma tadger... baws killin' me man... nae wonder the Highlands are deserted...

Robbie, Rhino and Mo look at each other.

ROBBIE

Whit did he say?

RHINO

Somethin' aboot his baws in the Highlands...

They shake their heads and walk on.

A LITTLE LATER: a strategic point, with a good view of an isolated set of buildings which includes a distillery and dunnage. Robbie, Mo and Rhino, munch on their sandwiches in silence.

> RHINO (CONT'D)
> Dae yi think he might have wandered intae a
> bog?

Shrugs between them.

They continue munching. At last Albert appears, crouched over slightly, and obviously in great discomfort.

> ALBERT
> Starvin'… palpa-fucking-tations in ma heart…
> [hands down his pants rearranging his tackle]
> chaffed bollocks… I am no very happy…

They are pissing themselves.

> RHINO
> 'Palpa-fuckin'-tations!'… Is that from your
> time as brain surgeon?

Albert reaches out to grab a sandwich but Mo pulls the bag away.

> MO
> Dirty bastard… wash yer hands first!

Albert collapses beside them at the end of his tether. Mo relents and hands him a sandwich.

> ALBERT
> But yi know whit really gets me… nae fucking
> plan!! [munching] Risking ma life fir fuck all!

RHINO

[Eyeballing Robbie] Right aboot that… Just
don't see how we can dae it… impossible…
middle of naewhere… we don't even hiv a
motor!

Robbie ignores them as he just stares at the distillery. He takes a
long drink from his bottle of Irn-Bru and lays it down.

MO

[To Robbie] Whit happened to your promise
tae Leonie… turning ower a new leaf and a'
that shit! Don't want yi taken cold feet halfway
through!

Robbie starts putting on his shoes and socks.

ROBBIE

Ah'm gonni keep ma promise… tae Leonie
and tae Luke… naebody is going tae lose out…
trust me…

They look at him in confusion.

ROBBIE (CONT'D)

Remember the donkey?

ALBERT

Ah still don't git that man…

ROBBIE

It's how yi see things… that's whit counts.
[Pause] We've got tae meet somebody… Ah
made an appointment before we left…

MO

Whit the fuck are you up tae!?

34. DISTILLERY

They walk through the distillery yard. Moments later a very friendly SECRETARY knocks politely on the manager's door.

> SECRETARY
> They're here... they do make you smile... They hitch-hiked the whole way from Glasgow!

Tasting room in the distillery:

The secretary and the distillery manager, DOBIE, walk through to the tasting room and confront the four of them who stand up as soon as he enters.

> MANAGER DOBIE
> Hello... quite a trip... so here we are...
> [feasting his eyes]... the Carntyne Malt Whisky club!

> ROBBIE
> Thanks for seeing us Mr Dobie... we're just newly set up... My name's Robbie... I'm the president... this here is Albert... financial secretary... Rhino... in charge of new membership... and Mo... social secretary and general procurement of whatever we need...

They are stunned and try to demonstrate the decorum fitting to their new found rank.

> MANAGER DOBIE
> So what can we do for you?

> ROBBIE
> We've read the reports... for us, the auction of a Malt Mill, is more important than landing on the moon...

The manager chuckles.

>   ROBBIE (CONT'D)
>   We've come to ask for your autograph…
>   and if it's possible… for our newsletter… a
>   photograph of you with the cask.

The others are amazed at his brass neck.

>   ROBBIE (CONT'D)
>   And only if it's not a bother… would you let
>   us witness the tasting with the Grand Master
>   of the Quaich, Mr Rory McAllister… we just
>   want tae be able to tell our grandkids… we
>   were there…

The boys stare at Robbie trying to hide their shock.

The manager is touched and looks at them in wonder, stuck for words.

>   SECRETARY
>   That's so sweet…

35. FIELD, BY DISTILLERY – DAY

In a field, with spectacular views to one side, and the distillery to the other, Mo and Rhino make a right mess of trying to put up the tent.

Albert tries to light a gas stove, while Robbie rummages about in his rucksack.

Albert eventually gets the stove on the go and carefully, delicately, lays a jumbo can of baked beans on the flame.

>   MO
>   [To Robbie] So sweet! Just canni believe
>   yi dragged us in there! Fucked up the best
>   opportunity o' our whole lives!

ROBBIE

Shut it… gi' me yir Irn-Bru bottles…

RHINO

They've even got oor photos…

MO

Wi ma record! Once they know it's gone…
Ah'm fucked! Thought yi were smart!

Robbie starts pouring out the remnants of their Irn-Bru bottles
which stops them all dead in their tracks. Then he starts rinsing
one out carefully with water from a big plastic bottle.

ROBBIE

Once they know?… [emptying and rinsing]…
They will never know… [confused] Nothing's
going tae go missing… naebody is going to
lose… a win–win situation for mankind…

MO

Have you gone mad?

ROBBIE

Did yi see those thin slats on the outside wall?

MO

Aye… did yi see the size o' those locks on the
fucking door?! The alarms… and the camera
fixed on the front door?

They watch, amazed, as Robbie takes out a roll of thin plastic
tubing from his rucksack and stretches it out.

ROBBIE

Aye, one camera, one alarm… but nane inside.
No even a security guard…

RHINO

How dae yi know?

ROBBIE

Ah asked the secretary… naebody steals anythin'
up here… ever… one road oot… dead end…
last reported theft here was wi the Vikings…

MO

Yi're forgettin'… one entrance wi a door as
thick as Albert's skull… are yi planning a tunnel
between noo and the morra?

ROBBIE

Nope. Ah walk in… [pause] then Ah walk oot.

Silence as they study him.

ALBERT

Here comes that fucking donkey again…

ROBBIE

During the tasting we a' stand at the back…
everybody will have their eyes glued to the
Grand Master… You guys cover me… Ah
simply drift in behind the barrels… hide there
the whole night… place locked up… during
the night you lot come wi the bottles…
[indicating tubing] Ah stick one end in the
barrel, the other through the slats to yous
outside away fae the camera… next day during
the auction and hullabaloo Ah drift back in…
join yis… enjoy the show… simple.

Silence as they look at each other.

MO

[Lighting up]… We only take four bottles…
and yi replace it wi whisky fae the best barrel
in the warehouse… that's why yi asked…

RHINO

And some rich cunt pays thousands…

ROBBIE

Fir something he'll never drink. And even
if he does… dae yi think he's gonni admit
making a prick o' himsel and hiv every
collector in the world pissin' themselves wi
delight?

Silence. They all look at each other in wonder. Mo stares at him
with admiration.

Albert is staring at the beans thinking.

ALBERT

Nae donkey?

ROBBIE

Nae donkey Albert.

ALBERT

[Solemn] Our time has come.

They stare at him in confusion.

ALBERT (CONT'D)

There comes a point in every man's life…

He continues to stir as the boys wait in exasperated silence for the
key to all knowledge. Still he stirs and stirs.

ALBERT (CONT'D)

And that point has come.

They shake their heads in resignation.

Robbie's phone rings. Robbie is taken aback.

ROBBIE

Dougie?… [in response to their confusion] Ma
flatmate…

Robbie walks off and listens. The boys can see he's agitated, and
now furious. He puts the phone back in his pocket and joins them.

RHINO

Clancy?

Robbie nods.

ROBBIE

Came roon lookin' fir me… Dougie's in the
hospital.

Robbie marches off to be by himself.

The sun begins to sink.

He sits on a rock and takes a deep breath to try and calm himself
as he looks at the distillery in the distance.

36. DISTILLERY, DUNNAGE, DAY

The dunnage has a stunning authentic atmosphere after storing
so much whisky for decade after decade. It has an other-worldly
feel; the smell too is distinctive. Black fungus, the 'champignon
ivrogne' that lives off the evaporating alcohol clings to the walls
and ceilings.

An area by the door has been carefully prepared, with the Malt
Mill cask, like the Holy Grail, mounted on a special wooden plinth.

It lies on its side with the bung facing upwards. On its side is the faint white mark of 'Malt Mill'.

A special raised stair and mount has been especially prepared in readiness for the auction the following day.

Robbie and co move to the back of the group. He looks out into the gloomy darkness as the long line of barrels (only three high) stretch way back into the dunnage.

Journalists, photographers, and potential bidders push to the front as the distillery manager Dobie and other top company officials move towards the cask. The two policemen drift in behind them, and face the crowd.

Robbie catches a glimpse of Thaddeus who approaches the Grand Master and they have a brief but friendly interchange.

> GRAND MASTER
> Ah Thaddeus... how badly does your client
> want this one?

> THADDEUS
> All depends on you Rory...

Thaddeus's sharp eyes spot Robbie. He's intrigued and moves towards him.

> THADDEUS (CONT'D)
> Hello Robbie... I hope you are not going to
> outbid me eh?

> ROBBIE
> You never know...

Thaddeus smiles and holds his eye for a moment before heading to the front as the Grand Master joins Dobie by the cask.

MANAGER DOBIE

Ladies and Gentlemen... May I present you
with the Grand Master of the Quaich... the
one and only Mr Rory McAllister!

Applause.

The cask is struck with the bung flogger by Dobie and the bung
is extracted.

Robbie stands behind his three mates and keeps an eye on the
two policemen facing the crowd.

With great theatricality the Grand Master is handed a special
nosing glass by a man wearing white gloves.

Next, Dobie is handed the long delicate instrument, the valinch,
which is used to extract whisky from barrels.

Dobie, with all the solemnity of an alter boy at the Vatican, inserts
the valinch inside the cask and very slowly, deliberately, without
spilling a drop, deposits an inch of the golden nectar inside the
Grand Master's nosing glass.

In a deadly silence, and with total reverence, the Grand Master
gently swirls the drink around his glass and looks for the tears
running down the side.

He noses the whisky for some time; his face can't but hide extreme
satisfaction.

Robbie can see the two policemen are riveted too.

Still total silence. Robbie takes a few steps back towards the barrels.

The Grand Master now holds it up to the light, swirls again, and
after another long hesitation, savouring the moment, he lifts it to
his lips and tastes.

He rolls the sample around his palate and shakes his head in respectful wonder.

He takes a breath and whispers…

GRAND MASTER
Uisge beatha… the water of life…

Total silence. Every eye is on him.

Robbie darts behind the barrels.

GRAND MASTER (CONT'D)
[Holding up the glass, photographers flash]
I think I may be one of the luckiest human
beings alive… this is without doubt an
authentic Malt Mill… incomparable… one of
the most magnificent drams I have ever had the
privilege to taste… whoever ends up with this
precious liquid will own perhaps the best malt
whisky ever made… [toasting] Slaite!

The Grand Master downs the rest.

A robust and elderly NORTH AMERICAN, wearing a baseball cap, studies the Grand Master with shrewd hard eyes.

NORTH AMERICAN
[Loud, above the hubbub] You bet your
reputation on it Mister?

GRAND MASTER
My life on it, Sir… I give you my word.

Thaddeus stares at Dobie who nods at him politely before replacing the wooden bung in the precious cask.

Rhino, Mo and Albert split to different sides of the assemblage so they don't draw attention as a group.

Robbie, tucked up behind a barrel, hears the sound of applause.

OUTSIDE THE DUNNAGE:

The crowd stream out, including Rhino, Mo and Albert. Albert's jaw drops as he sees one of the policemen beckoning him over.

Albert points at himself as Mo and Rhino glance at each other nervously. The policeman nods. Albert, trying to keep his nerve moves closer.

> POLICEMAN
> So you can tell me... what's the tartan?

> ALBERT
> McKinnon... after ma grandma...

> POLICEMAN
> Nice one.

> ALBERT
> Thanks Chief.

INSIDE THE DUNNAGE:

Robbie, from in between barrels way back, spies on the last remaining figures inside the dunnage.

The auctioneer, and his four assistants, make the final preparations as Dobie waits to lock up. A young policeman is also with them.

The AUCTIONEER checks his gavel from his heightened position at the podium. His four assistants are all on mobiles as the auctioneer waits for their reports. They wind up.

> POLICEMAN
> Expecting phone bids too?

                            AUCTIONEER
          An equity fund in New York, an agent in Hong
          Kong representing some big wig in China…
          two from Moscow and one from Delhi… there
          is an outside chance of a bid from Brazil but
          still waiting to confirm…

He's amazed.

They switch off the lights and head out. Dobie closes the thick
wooden doors. Robbie can hear the locks turn.

The voices and footsteps disappear.

Robbie crawls from underneath the barrels.

He turns on his torch, and then wraps the elasticated strap round
his head to leave his arms free. The beam lights up the cask before
him and the faded words 'Malt Mill'.

37. THE TENT – NIGHT

Mo, chewing gum, Rhino and Albert wait by their tent, faces lit
by their torches, overlooking the distillery.

In the distance they can see a bar in the village street, light pouring
from its windows.

They can hear the sound of a ceilidh band in full swing.

                            RHINO
          Can we…

                            MO
          [Cutting them off] Naw!

                            ALBERT
          Even fir a…

MO

Naw!

Albert and Rhino look at each other.

ALBERT

The French lassies could be in there… can we
just…

MO

Go and practice yer French?

RHINO

Two minutes Mo… just tae say hello…

ALBERT

Yi can hiv the tent tae yersel… yi know whit
ma feet are like…

MO

Unbelievable… on the day that could change
oor lives for ever… a' yi can think aboot is
rampant sex wi' strangers… Am Ah right?

They look at each other sheepishly.

Mo receives a text. She reads it quickly.

MO (CONT'D)

Robbie… let's go [spitting out the gum]… pair
o' cocks…

They jump up and swing down the hill.

38. DUNNAGE:

Robbie, with the torch still on his forehead, peers outside from one slat to another.

He listens intently. Silence.

He moves over to the cask and caresses it with his hand.

He tries to remove the wooden bung with his hand, but it is in too tight. The flogger and the valinch have been placed underneath the cask on a little shelf on the plinth.

Hesitating, with his heart beating, Robbie strikes the flogger against the cask several times.

It sounds deafening in the deadly silence. The bung pops out. He lifts it off easily, and then extracts the piece of cloth gauze too which enveloped the wooden bung, and lays both carefully on the barrel.

Robbie listens carefully. Still silence.

He puts his nose to the hole and breathes deeply. It takes his breath away.

He quickly grabs his backpack and pulls out the long piece of thin plastic tubing.

He inserts one end carefully inside the barrel and then tapes it firm against the cask.

He expertly unrolls it and moves some 20 yards to one of the narrow slats.

ALBERT
Uisge Beatha!!

Robbie jumps out of his skin.

ROBBIE

Fuck... ma heart! [passing tube through the
slat] Mo, take that... keep it low... and start
sucking... hiv the bottles ready... let's go...
and don't spill a drop! And nae floaters mind...

Robbie heads back to the cask.

His heart races as he sees the golden liquid rise up through the
plastic tube. He follows its progress towards the slat.

He leans against the wall, his face in wonder, as the liquid now
climbs the slope to the slat, up and down like a heartbeat from
each suck, and then, from outside, the most glorious sound he's
ever heard. Gentle drops of liquid gush into glass.

He smiles to himself and closes his eyes for a moment as he tries
to stay calm.

OUTSIDE: Rhino holds a tiny torch which focusses on the fourth
Irn-Bru bottle half-filled with Malt Mill.

Still the magical sound of liquid splashing gently into the bottle.

MO

[Whispering]... That's the fourth Robbie!

Albert, on lookout, suddenly see the lights of a car approach the
building. He waves at them in alarm.

RHINO

[Whispered] Fuck! Someone coming... hide
Robbie! We're off!

Robbie sprints to the barrel as a car parks outside and the doors
slam.

He pulls out the tube nipping the end with his finger as voices become audible and a lock is undone. He grabs the bung and squeezes it in as tight as he can with his weight as the last lock is undone.

He swipes his bag from the floor and sprints for cover along the side of the dunnage (still gripping the tubing) a mere second before the door swings open.

The lights go on.

Thaddeus and Dobie move over to the cask.

Dobie looks down at the cask and notices the thin little bit of gauze lying on top of the barrel. He picks it up, and looks at Thaddeus. He's alert and starts to walk down the narrow space between the two halves of the dunnage, his eyes darting along each row.

He stands in silence. Listening. Nothing.

He walks back towards Thaddeus.

> MANAGER DOBIE
> Can't believe I left that out… must be the
> nerves…

He stares out over the dunnage.

He hits the cask with the flogger and the bung pops out.

OUTSIDE THE DUNNAGE: The boys crouch down.

INSIDE THE DUNNAGE: Dobie drops a tiny measure of whisky into Thaddeus's nosing glass.

Thaddeus smells it, and then tastes it. He shakes his head in wonder.

                    THADDEUS
         Thank you Angus… thank you… I'll die a
         happy man…

                 MANAGER DOBIE
         Breaks my heart to see it go… not a word eh…

Nosing again between the pair of them for a few long moments.

                    THADDEUS
         And my little suggestion Angus… [looking
         round the dunnage] Who would ever know?

Dobie stares at him long and hard. Thaddeus can see him falter.

               THADDEUS (CONT'D)
         It's a win-win situation… nobody loses…

Robbie's face is frozen in amazement. Dobie seems to struggle.

               THADDEUS (CONT'D)
         My client only wants… one bottle to keep, one
         to swap… and one to drink with his friends…
         Don't think we can match the American…

                 MANAGER DOBIE
         But provenance!? He must want proof…

Thaddeus smiles.

                    THADDEUS
         Not a stickler for detail…

                 MANAGER DOBIE
         At that price!

                    THADDEUS
         A drop in the ocean…

Dobie shakes his head in amazement.

> MANAGER DOBIE
> He knows… that's enough…

Thaddeus nods. Dobie is stunned as the choice presses on him.

> THADDEUS
> Between me, you and these four walls… a little
> nest egg.

Long pause as he genuinely struggles.

> MANAGER DOBIE
> I don't have the nerve…

He picks up the bung, replaces the gauze, and hammers the bung into the barrel.

Robbie holds his breath.

OUTSIDE THE DUNNAGE: Thaddeus and Dobie emerge and lock the door.

LATER: INSIDE THE DUNNAGE: Robbie skilfully finishes off draining whisky from another fine old barrel into his Irn-Bru bottle at the other end of the dunnage.

In turn, he takes that over to the Malt Mill cask, and carefully transfers the whisky from the bottle.

This time he takes extreme care to wrap the gauze around the bung before he replaces it. (He places his jumper over the bung before hitting it with the flogger.)

He crawls back to his hiding place at the far end of the dunnage. From his breast pocket he takes out a small sampling bottle (that fits in a fist) with a cork on top.

He smells it and smiles to himself.

39. DISTILLERY

The sun rises over the distinctive pagoda-style roofs of the old distillery.

Perfect silence, apart from the sound of seagulls and distant sound of the ocean from the Firth.

40. DUNNAGE – MORNING

> AUCTIONEER
> Who will open the bidding at five hundred thousand pounds?!

Applause from some of the onlookers.

> AUCTIONEER (CONT'D)
> Silence please!... five hundred thousand!

The dunnage is even more packed than at the tasting.

The auctioneer is in full swing, and the excitement from the onlookers is only matched by the stress of the central players.

The main bidders, which includes Thaddeus (with an ear to his mobile), four North Americans, three Russians, three Chinese, a few Scots and half a dozen miscellaneous dealers of various nationalities who have prime position in front of the auctioneer on his mounted pedestal.

To one side the Grand Master, Dobie and the two policemen stand together riveted by the activities.

Towards the back are various onlookers, whisky company officials, press, and right at the back, Rhino, Albert and Mo.

The auctioneer's four assistants are down below him, each one with an ear to their mobile taking bids from outside the country.

AUCTIONEER (CONT'D)
[Indicating the bidder with a nod] 510, 520,
530, 540, 550, 560, 570, 580, 590, 600…

The gang look at each other in amazement. They look around for
Robbie but there is no sign of him.

MO
Where the fuck is he?

Thaddeus, who still hasn't bid yet, whispers on the phone, while
studying the faces of those around him.

AUCTIONEER
[Glancing at his assistants] 610, [to Chinese] 620, [Russian] 630,
[suited agent] 640, [to assistant on phone] 650,000… 660?

The Chinese and American who had been bidding bail out with
the briefest shake of their heads.

AUCTIONEER (CONT'D)
660 anyone? 660 once… 660 twice…

Another North American makes a bid.

AUCTIONEER (CONT'D)
670…

It sets off another gush of bids from new players. Still Thaddeus
watches.

AUCTIONEER (CONT'D)
680… [Assistant with phone] 680, 690, 690…
do we have 7?

The excitement sweeps the dunnage.

A barely noticeable nod from an older Chinese man who hasn't
bid before.

AUCTIONEER (CONT'D)
I have 700... 700 thousand pounds...

The gang are stunned.

RHINO
Jesus, where is he?

AUCTIONEER
Do I have 710? [The previous American shakes
his head, as does his assistant with the phone]
Do I have 710 anyone?... 710? 710?

Various bidders shake their heads.

AUCTIONEER (CONT'D)
Seven hundred and ten thousand pounds
sterling once... twice... [he lifts the gavel]...

Now the North American with the baseball cap (recognisable
from the tasting) puts up his hand.

AUCTIONEER (CONT'D)
I have 710... 720 [the last Chinese bidder pulls
out, but new faces come in] 730, 740 [from
North American], 750... Do I have 750? 750
anyone... anyone 750... 740 once... 740
twice...

Other hands go up.

AUCTIONEER (CONT'D)
I have 750... 760...

Other bidders pull out, but not the American with the cap.

They rattle through at speed, the American and another Chinese
bidder.

AUCTIONEER (CONT'D)
760... 770... 780... 790... do I have 800? I
do... 800!

Another wave of excitement as Thaddeus listens carefully on his phone.

Through the crowd the gang see Robbie moving over behind the Grand Master and Dobie, right beside NEIL the policeman. Robbie nods at the policeman and shakes his hand. He then turns round to grin at them.

MO
[Grinning too] What a brass neck!

They can hardly contain their delight as the action continues.

AUCTIONEER
810, 20, 30, 40, 50, 60, 70, 80, 90... 900
thousand pounds... 910, 20, 30, 40, 50, 60, 70,
80 [the American nods] 990... Do I have one
million pounds!?

Another wave of tension; the auctioneer looks at Thaddeus who still whispers on his phone. He in turn stares across at the American.

AUCTIONEER (CONT'D)
Do I have one million?...[Thaddeus hesitates,
sweating] Do I have one million... [Thaddeus
nods] One million!

Applause breaks out.

AUCTIONEER (CONT'D)
Do I have one million and ten?

The American stares at Thaddeus. A long moment between them.

AUCTIONEER (CONT'D)

One million once, one million twice…

He raises his gavel.

AUCTIONEER (CONT'D)

[American nods] One million 10, 20, 30, 40,
50…

Thaddeus whispers on phone and nods.

AUCTIONEER (CONT'D)

Yes… I have one million sixty [looking at
American] Do I have 70?

The American is deadly still and again turns to face a stony
Thaddeus.

AUCTIONEER (CONT'D)

Do I have one million seventy?… [American
nods] Yes… I do… [Thaddeus] 80…
[American] 90… Do I have one million one
hundred thousand pounds… [to Thaddeus] Do
I have one million one hundred thousand, Sir?

Robbie stares at him as Thaddeus whispers in Russian on the
mobile. The pressure tells.

Thaddeus looks up and catches Robbie gently shaking his head.
It distracts and confuses him for a moment. He gets instructions
and nods.

AUCTIONEER (CONT'D)

One million one hundred thousand pounds!

Thaddeus catches Robbie shaking his head again.

AUCTIONEER (CONT'D)

[To American] Do I have one million one
hundred and ten?

145

The North American and Thaddeus stare at each other. The American nods.

> AUCTIONEER (CONT'D)
> One million one hundred and ten thousand…
> do I have 20?

Thaddeus takes his last instructions. He looks up at the American. No movement.

> AUCTIONEER (CONT'D)
> One million one hundred and ten thousand
> pounds once… twice… [looking at Thaddeus,
> nothing.]

He smashes the gavel down on his podium.

> AUCTIONEER (CONT'D)
> [Pointing to American] Gone to the gentlemen
> over there! I do believe, Sir, that is a world
> record!

Chaos. Wild clapping, especially among the gang. The press jump in and try to get a photo.

The American heads over to a devastated looking Thaddeus. They shake hands.

> THADDEUS
> Many many congratulations…

> AMERICAN
> Thank you… thank you… thank you… could
> I ask who your client is?

> THADDEUS
> I don't even know his name…

AMERICAN
His country?

THADDEUS
From Moscow… that's all I know…

The American smiles in deep satisfaction.

AMERICAN
Fucked the Ruskies once again!!!

More of a media scramble. The Grand Master and Dobie are called over to get their photograph taken with the American by his cask.

PRESS
[Shouts] You must have one little taste Sir!

Robbie's eyes follow Thaddeus who makes his way out still on the mobile.

Thaddeus does a double take as he spots Robbie again, but has to continue his urgent conversation.

Robbie catches a glimpse of the North American getting a sample from his precious cask.

Robbie joins the gang who watch with great trepidation.

MO
Ah fuck… this is it.

The American gets his dram and holds it up for the cameras.

He notices the gang in their kilts, transfixed, studying them from the back.

AMERICAN
You young Scotch kids!… Come up and join
me please for this historic moment!

They oblige and crowd round.

JOURNALIST
You have to taste it! Tell us what it's like!

The American stares at the glass and takes a sip. Silence for a few long moments.

The gang are crapping themselves.

He takes another sip. He looks down at the glass again, and then up at the press.

AMERICAN
Bonnie Scatland!!! God bless you all!

GANG
[Punching the air, bouncing] 'Bonnie Scotland!
Bonnie Scotland! We'll support you ever
more... We'll support you ever more... Bonnie
Scotland...'

Some of the onlookers join in.

The photographs flash as the gang now double up in mirth.

41. VISITORS' CENTRE – DAY

Thaddeus, with a whisky before him, is at the bar drowning his sorrows along with a few other journalists and onlookers from the grand event.

Robbie appears at the entrance and studies him for a moment. He approaches and pulls up a stool beside him.

ROBBIE
Commiserations...

Thaddeus takes his hand and smiles.

THADDEUS

My client gets what he wants... always... not
best pleased I can tell you...

Robbie leans across and takes one of the clean nosing glasses lined
up on the bar.

ROBBIE

[Quietly] It's really 'congratulations'... on not
throwing a million smackers down the pan...

Now he has his attention. Robbie takes the glass and pulls out a
sampling bottle from his breast pocket. He pours the whisky into
Thaddeus's glass and pushes it over.

Thaddeus looks at it. He noses the glass and his eyes suddenly
flash at Robbie.

THADDEUS

[Stunned] Oh my God... My God! I don't
believe it.

They grin at each other. Thaddeus tastes. Shakes his head, then
chuckles.

THADDEUS (CONT'D)

How much have you got?

ROBBIE

One to keep... one to swap... one to drink
with friends.

Thaddeus stares at him in wonder.

THADDEUS

You didn't do a deal with Dobie?

Robbie shakes his head.

> ROBBIE
>
> Hasn't got the nerve.

> THADDEUS
>
> [Admiration] You little bastard... I'll be
> damned... [Pause] How much do you want?

> ROBBIE
>
> Two hundred grand...

> THADDEUS
>
> With no provenance! Not a chance...

> ROBBIE
>
> Not a stickler for detail... that's what Ah heard.

Thaddeus chuckles and shakes his head in amazement.

> ROBBIE (CONT'D)
>
> But that's not all. [Holding his eye] Ah want a
> job. A real job.

42. EAST END, GLASGOW – DAY

Robbie, Rhino, Mo and Albert (still a bit crouched) walk along
a busy road still wearing their kilts and carrying their rucksacks.

A police car drives past on the other side and Rhino clocks it
immediately. He can see a face peering at him in wonder from
inside the car.

> RHINO
>
> Fuck me! It's Plod! Hates my guts!

The police car has pulled into the middle of the road and against
busy traffic is looking for a place to do a U-turn to get back to
them.

MO

Make a run fir it noo!

ROBBIE

Naebody moves!

RHINO

Robbie. Let's go… they won't catch us a'!

ROBBIE

[Vicious] Naebody fucking moves!… Keep yer
nerve… and mind yer manners.

The police car pulls up beside them and the enormous lanky
policeman gets out of the car with a grin as wide as the Clyde.

POLICEMAN 1

[Staring at Rhino] 'Oh yes… it's the big
wanking Beanpole!'

ROBBIE

Good afternoon Constable.

POLICEMAN 1

Hello ladies… a little country dancing eh? [to
Mo] What the hell have you been robbing Ms
Stone?

The Beanpole nods at his colleague who begins to search them
as the Beanpole moves to the car to make a call to see if there are
any outstanding arrest warrants etc.

Their private belongings are carefully placed in front of each
rucksack on the pavement. By each rucksack is one unopened
bottle of Irn-Bru.

RADIO

All four are currently carrying out Community
Service Orders… attendance is fine…
behaviour fine…

POLICEMAN 2

Nothing.

The tall police officer joins his partner and stares at them all again.
He's convinced they have been up to something and he virtually
x-rays them.

He bends down and flicks through their belongings again. He
turns a pair of Albert's socks inside out – and his body wilts with
the reek.

As he rummages through Robbie's stuff he accidentally hits the
bottle of Irn-Bru and it tumbles over, only to land on the towel.

POLICEMAN 1

Excuse me.

He picks it up and balances it right way up again.

The gang glance at each other.

POLICEMAN 2

Okay let's go…

The taller policeman continues to stare at them. In his bones he
knows they have been up to mischief.

POLICEMAN 1

Okay girls… catch you later, so to speak.

The policemen head for the car. The gang, hearts beating, take a
sigh of relief.

The Beanpole clicks his fingers with a moment of inspiration, and
turns back to them.

POLICEMAN 1 (CONT'D)

Right… think I forgot?!

He moves over to them, eyes shining. Rhino seems ready to run for it again.

POLICEMAN 1 (CONT'D)
Up with your kilts!

The three boys look at each other nervously, as the Policeman indicates Mo should turn her eyes.

The boys shake their heads.

ALBERT
Yi'll never sleep again officer…

ROBBIE
Have yi made your confession?

RHINO
Every time yi hiv yer breakfast…

POLICEMAN 1
Shut it!! [Pause] Up I said!

The three boys, together, grab the hems of their kilts.

Now on the policeman's face. His face contorts in near physical pain.

POLICEMAN 2
You should get some ointment on that son.

POLICEMAN
[Barely getting the words out] Turn round for God's sake…

Now three translucent white arses reflect the sun and all but blind the forces of law and order.

POLICEMAN (CONT'D)
[To the other] Should have brought ma
welding mask…

POLICEMAN 2
And a sick bag.

The policemen get into their car and head off.

Mo and Albert, side by side, pick up their bottles. While the others
are relieved, Albert has stirred himself up to be an indignant citizen
in the face of totalitarian repression.

ALBERT
Fuckin' polis man… molestin' innocent
civilians… [now brandishing his bottle above
his head] We shall not be moved! Robert
the Bruce! Billy Connolly! Braveheart! Alex
Ferguson! We are the fuckin' champions!!

He swings round to Mo and with clumsy gusto smacks his bottle
against hers.

ALBERT
Cheers.

Their bottles clash and smash… Mo's is on the ground in pieces.

Albert holds the top half of his broken bottle.

They stare at the puddle of precious Malt Mill on the ground.

RHINO
Pair o' fucking morons!!… That's your share…
up the spout… yis are gettin' fuck all!

Robbie leans up against the wall and slides down to his hunkers.

154

Albert stares at his half-broken bottle, still in his hand, as Malt Mill dribbles down his sleeve. He licks a taste from his wet hand.

                    MO
          That's the story o' ma life…

Albert, terrified of their reaction, stares at the broken bottle.

Long silence as they all glance at Robbie. He is still on his hunkers, with his fingers pinching the bridge of his nose. Eyes shut. He tries to calm himself.

Albert nervously clears his throat.

                    ALBERT
          Can Ah just say…

                    RHINO
          [Whisper] Shut the fuck up Albert…

                    ALBERT
          Just a little point…

                    RHINO
          [Building] Gonnie ring yer fucking neck!

                    MO
          Best be quiet Albert…

                    ALBERT
          Teeny weenie tiny wee point…

Rhino jumps towards him but Mo holds him back.

                    RHINO
          Nail yer baws tae yer skull if yi don't shut it!

                    ALBERT
          It's the last thing Ah'll ever say tae yis…
          [pause, he has their attention]… now don't get
          angry…

RHINO

[Internal] Angry… he's killin' me!

Silence.

ALBERT

Listen… if there were only four bottles left in the entire world… that makes them very very precious… right?

RHINO

Yes you fucking giant numptie!

ALBERT

But!… but… if there's only two bottles left in the entire world… that makes them even mair very very precious!

All the boys stop dead.

ALBERT (CONT'D)

Common sense… supply and demand and a' that…

Robbie opens his eyes for the first time.

He stares at Albert.

They all look at each other. It sinks in.

Robbie looks back at Albert's expectant face.

Robbie begins to chuckle and shakes his head in wonder.

All three start pissing themselves as Albert lets out an enormous grin of satisfaction.

ALBERT (CONT'D)

Ah had it a' planned man. Smash!

The sound of text on Robbie's phone. It shuts them up. Mo can tell by his face.

                    MO

        Clancy?

                    ROBBIE

        [Reading] Tick tock tick tock.

Robbie stares ahead of him.

43. EAST END STREETS TO TANNING SALON, GLASGOW

Robbie sits in the back seat of a car beside Rhino and Mo. Albert sits in the front seat beside the driver, one of their mates.

Robbie is deadly quiet, withdrawn into himself.

They follow a Passat VW full of young men from a safe distance.

                    ALBERT

        [Peering] Slow doon... no too close. Think
        there's four... Clancy's there for definite...
        Sniper tae.

Robbie's eyes flash. Robbie pulls the flick knife (the one he took from Sniper) from his pocket. He flicks the button and the knife snaps open. He puts it back in his pocket again.

                    DRIVER

        Ah don't like this man... he's a fuckin'
        psycho...

The Passat turns into Duke street, and their car follows.

The Passat suddenly swerves across the road and parks on the other side of the street facing the traffic.

ROBBIE

Pull in!

Robbie's car pulls into the left some 35 yards down from them.

Clancy [in distinctive leather jacket] and Sniper jump out of the car as Clancy talks briefly to the driver. More chat, and Sniper jumps back into the car again.

RHINO

Fuck me… he's headin' for the sunbeds!

Clancy turns and heads for the tanning 'boutique'. The RECEPTIONIST is outside the door having a smoke. Clancy exchanges words with her. She continues smoking as Clancy heads inside.

ROBBIE

[To driver] Hiv yi got a tyre lever in the boot?

The boys glance at each other nervously.

DRIVER

Aye.

Clancy's car takes off. As Robbie gets out, Rhino makes to follow.

ROBBIE

On ma own.

RHINO

No way! He's fuckin' crazy…

ROBBIE

On ma own!

Robbie slams the door shut, opens the boot, and spots a tyre lever among the tools, and slips it up his sleeve. He shuts the boot and heads across the road.

The boutique is on a corner with tall windows. He looks up at garish sign. 'TANERIFE'. He turns to look at his mates, and impatiently indicates they should drive off. They eventually do.

He heads towards the entrance. The receptionist still smokes outside, but now chats on her mobile too. She indicates he should go inside.

RECEPTIONIST
[Aside to Robbie] Use whit one yi like...
there's only one in use... gi me five...

Robbie nods and heads inside and closes the door. His eyes scan the cubicle doors.

One cubicle door is closed. Robbie moves over and listens outside. Silence apart from the distant sound of music.

He quietly slips the lever from inside his left arm. He tests the door. It is locked. He gently slips the lever between door and frame. He snaps it open and bursts in sharply.

Silence, apart from the slightly louder music from inside the beaming sunbed.

Clancy's clothes and leather jacket hang from the wall, with his shoes below. Robbie gently moves towards the sunbed. He lays down the crowbar and takes the knife from his pocket and flicks it open.

He gently leans forward and eases open the sunbed.

Clancy lies there with a pair of mini paper pants protecting his glory, with eye pads protecting his eyes, and an iPod pumping loudly into earphones.

Robbie stands over him for a second or two. He examines the ugly scars and wounds he has on different parts of his body, not unlike his own, and his feet moving to the beat of the music.

He stretches out the knife and carefully gets the blade under the edge of the paper pants and then flicks it up in a flash.

CLANCY

[Screaming] Fuck!!!!!!

He sits up in a shot snapping mask and earphones from his head. Robbie has the knife under his chin; with his left hand Robbie indicates he should lie down again.

Stunned he does so, and covers up his bollocks.

ROBBIE

Tick tock tick tock.

It sends a shudder of fear across Clancy's eyes.

CLANCY

Fuck dae you want?

Robbie, hard as nails, just stares at him as Clancy's nerves mount. The knife gently presses a fraction harder on his throat.

Clancy swallows nervously.

Robbie puts a hand into his pocket which makes Clancy even more fearful. Robbie hands him something. He takes it nervously with one hand. It is a photograph of a baby. It confuses him and his eyes dart back to Robbie.

ROBBIE

That little baby saved your life.

Clancy is still perplexed.

ROBBIE (CONT'D)

His name is Luke. Ma son.

Robbie stares at him.

CLANCY

Yi'r no gonni dae me?

ROBBIE

Fir the first time in ma life… Ah've got
something tae lose… If yi don't let me take
care o' Luke… or yi hurt one more o' ma
mates… Ah'm gonni find yi again… [fierceness
in his eye, the blade presses on his throat even
harder] and Ah'm gonni slit yer throat.

He means every word.

ROBBIE (CONT'D)

Dae yi understand that?

Clancy's hard eyes calculate.

ROBBIE (CONT'D)

[Pressing] Dae yi?

He nods.

In a sudden move Robbie points the knife at a deep scar on
Clancy's side.

ROBBIE (CONT'D)

Is that mine?

CLANCY

Aye…

Robbie pulls up his T-shirt and shows him a similar scar on his
chest.

CLANCY (CONT'D)

That mine?

ROBBIE

Aye…

Robbie drops the knife to his side. He steps back.

ROBBIE (CONT'D)

Time we called it quits.

They look each other in the eye for a few moments.

Robbie heads to the door and then turns. He holds his eye for a second.

ROBBIE (CONT'D)

Funny… Ah could be you. You could be me.
One in a box… one in a cell… or we could
just walk oot o' here… and live a life… [Pause]
Good luck.

He turns and walks out. Robbie wanders along the street. For the first time we see a lightness in his eyes.

44. SIDESTREET, OUTSIDE A BAR – DAY

Robbie, Rhino, Albert and Mo walk down a side street and stop outside a modest bar, with frosted glass above the eyeline so those outside can't see in.

ROBBIE (CONT'D)

[Deadly serious] Thaddeus is gonni go
mental… don't want yous windin' him up…
stay here and don't attract any attention to
yerselves… right…

Robbie enters the bar as the other three look at each other sheepishly. Rhino turns to the window and tries to peer in but he can't see a thing.

ALBERT

Canni stand the tension man... [to Rhino]
Bend doon... lemme on yer shoulders...

RHINO

Fuck off...

MO

Go oan... he's right... canni stand it either...

Rhino gives in, bends down, and with Mo's help clambers onto
Rhino's shoulders. Albert, balancing precariously, cups his hands
round his eyes and peers though the window and commentates
on the action to Rhino and Mo below him.

ALBERT

Duznie look a happy bunny... no, no...
definitely no amused...

MO

Who fir fuck's sake?

ALBERT

Thaddeus!... In fact, Ah'd say he wuz aboot to
take a heart attack...

RHINO

Nae wonder... whit aboot Robbie?

ALBERT

He's pointin' the finger... on the attack... but
showin' signs o' distress Ah'd say...

RHINO

Me tae... stop movin' ya fat bastard...

MO

Maybe he just duznie believe him?

ALBERT

Gone quieter... Shhh!... There's been a
development...

MO

Whit the fuck does that mean?

ALBERT

A Checkpoint Charlie moment...

RHINO AND MO

Whit?!

ALBERT

A fuckin' exchange o' packages!... What else
could it mean?... Fuck me... looking good...
just shook hands! Just given Robbie something
else tae... On their way oot... here they
come...

He crashes down and lands on his arse just as Thaddeus and
Robbie come out of the bar.

Thaddeus stops to stare at them for a moment, taking them all in.
He shakes his head.

THADDEUS

[To Robbie, resigned] I believe every word...

He about turns and walks off with his briefcase in his hand.

Robbie walks over to them, and holds some magazine photos in
his hand. They all look at him with worried faces.

Robbie taps the inside of his jacket and smiles.

ROBBIE

Relax. It's a' here... we'll divide it up later!

                    MO
[Stunned] Can't believe it…

                    RHINO
Furious eh?

Robbie nods.

                    ROBBIE
Take it or leave it… A Malt Mill.

They begin to chuckle.

                    MO
[Nodding at folded up magazine pages] What's
that?

                    ROBBIE
[Handing it over] Look…

She does and stares down at a double spread of glossy photos
from a magazine. An older man, grizzled face but open smile,
turns barley inside a warehouse. (Perhaps other photos, by a kiln
or copper still that suggest artisanship and skill.) In the last, he's
leaning on a barrel and sipping a glass of the golden nectar.

                    ALBERT
So who's the old geezer?

                    ROBBIE
A friend o'Thaddeus… runs a distillery…

Confusion on their faces.

                    ROBBIE (CONT'D)
He's going tae take me on… teach me!

                    MO
Fantastic man…

ALBERT

[Shaking his head]… Yi'll be up some lonely
mountain… turn intae a sheep shagger…

ROBBIE

Na… no far fae Stirling… we'll git a wee flat
there in the city…

MO

[Touched for him] That's brilliant man…

They all shake his hand. Robbie grabs the photos again and stares
at them.

ROBBIE

[Almost to himself] A job…

MO

Does Leonie know?

ROBBIE

[Smiling at the thought] No yet… she'll be
over the moon.

RHINO

Whit aboot yer sentence?

ROBBIE

Ah'll be able tae finish it there at the
weekends… big Harry organised the transfer…

RHINO

Brilliant…

MO

Still canni believe he payed a' that dosh fir just
two bottles…

                    ROBBIE

   One bottle. [Pointing at Albert] Supply and
   demand wee man…

They are gobsmacked.

                    RHINO
   Where's the other one?

                    ROBBIE
   Ah need yer help guys wi one last thing…

45. HARRY'S FLAT

Harry makes his way up the close to his flat carrying some
shopping. He opens his door and heads into the kitchen.

The kitchen window is wide open, and the curtain undulates
in a light breeze. He's suddenly alert. He closes it down and
suspiciously starts looking round the flat.

He stops at the sitting room door. He stares at a simple bottle
with golden liquid without any label sitting in the middle of his
little table.

There is an envelope beside it.

He picks up the bottle and holds it up to the light.

He opens the envelope and pulls out a card, plus £500 in notes,
and then a folded up cutting from a newspaper.

The card is of a stunning view of the Highlands.

He turns it over, and whispers to himself as he reads.

                    HARRY
   Malt Mill… Angels' Share. [Pause] Thanks for
   giving me a chance… Robbie.

He's stunned.

He quickly unfolds the newspaper.

He stares in wonder at the full page photograph of the gang, faces elated, jumping around the American as he holds up his whisky by the famous cask. Headline, 'Highland auction breaks whisky world record'.

> HARRY (CONT'D)
> Ah'll be damned…

He punches the table and bursts out laughing in total delight.

He picks up the bottle and just stares at it as the chuckles gurgle up again.

He undoes the cork and smells it. Bliss. He shakes his head in wonder.

> HARRY (CONT'D)
> Angels' Share…

46. A LANE BEHIND LEONIE'S FAMILY HOME – DAY

Rhino, Mo and Albert stand in a back lane which runs along behind the gardens of a set of sandstone houses, one of which belongs to Leonie's parents.

A few bags are laid out by the gate into the garden.

A VW camper van turns the corner and makes it way up the lane, with lights flashing.

Robbie drives up.

> ALBERT
> Leonie… he's here! Look at this man!

She comes running out of the back door holding Luke.

The VW stops before her and she stands there amazed. She is shining, but still wary.

Robbie kisses both her and Luke.

> ROBBIE
>
> Whit dae yi think?

> LEONIE
>
> Can't believe it… where did you get it?

> ROBBIE
>
> Goes wi the job.

> LEONIE
>
> A VW camper van!

The boys glance at each other and know he's in trouble.

> RHINO
>
> Has to visit a' these distilleries… cheaper than
> an hotel…

> ALBERT
>
> Fucking cutbacks man… disgraceful.

They start piling in all the stuff bit by bit as Leonie places Luke in a baby seat.

At last Robbie and Leonie get in.

> ROBBIE
>
> Right… thanks guys… we'll git yis over once
> we're settled…

> ALBERT
>
> Don't let a' that fresh air wear yi doon…

> MO
>
> Good luck Robbie… we'll really miss yi.

ROBBIE

[Embracing Mo] Don't spend it a' in the slot
machines eh…

They hug affectionately. All of them.

Rhino, Robbie, and Mo wave off Robbie and Leonie.

Leonie is crying as she looks out at her house. She waves to the
threesome through her tears.

The VW takes off and disappears round a corner. Albert, Rhino
and Mo look forlorn.

They sit on the wall by the gardens for several long moments.

RHINO

Got tae hand it tae him… a bird, a wean, a
motor…

ALBERT

And a job.

RHINO

A fucking real job.

Long pause as they all nod and appreciate. They sink back into
themselves.

MO

Whit noo?

The three of them sit on the wall in silence.

ALBERT

Plenty o' dosh… Fuck it… let's get wasted…

They all look at each other for a moment and shrug.

They jump off the wall and head up the road.

47. COUNTRY ROAD – DAY

The VW, in the inside lane, is overtaken by every vehicle. Beautiful mountain scenery surrounds them.

INSIDE: Robbie drives the VW.

Robbie and Leonie stare ahead with enormous grins on their faces.

Leonie turns to check Luke who is asleep in his seat. He is. A moment of bliss.

She turns to look at Robbie. She stares at him for several long moments. [His scar side.]

> LEONIE
>
> Yi're a scamp Robbie Emmerson… from the
> first day I saw yi…

He turns to look at her, deadly serious, and then gives her a wink.

FROM OUTSIDE: The VW passes another glorious spot and disappears into the horizon.

FADE TO BLACK.

Appendix 1:

At the back of the court are public benches; this area is divided from the court by a waist-height wooden wall, and is packed by those awaiting sentencing, their families and friends.

It has a Dickensian feel; obvious from the faces, pinched skin, hairstyles, tracksuits, accents, and general demeanour of the public that there is an enormous class difference on either side of the dividing wooden wall. It is clear many have never worked, and probably never will. Several have scars on their faces. Some look dozy from their methadone prescriptions.

The Sheriff will have already read the social work enquiry report and suggestion for disposal by the social worker. The Procurator Fiscal will give a summary of the events, and thereafter the defence lawyer will make his plea in mitigation. Thereafter, the Sheriff will make up his mind as to disposal, i.e. dismissal, custodial sentence, or in these cases, a Community Service Order which requires the sentenced to carry out supervised work in the community as an alternative to custody.

Appendix 2:

Thaddeus was trained as a corporate lawyer, but was drawn far too much to the limelight to hang about in an office. He drifted into being a whisky broker, as both enthusiast and entrepreneur, before finding his niche with the super wealthy. His luxury flat in London is a mischievous hubbub and haven for the posh, but carefully mixed with the super nouveau riche, both domestic and foreign. He is at ease with wealth.

He has the sophistication, taste, and temperament to give confidence to the seriously rich navigating their way through the Capital who lack confidence in buying the extreme luxury 'items' only the very rich can buy; from art, to of course, the finest malts. He is a freelance agent, fixer, opportunist, advisor, counsellor par excellence. He knows Arab princes by their first name, and of course, can get tickets for a Chelsea game at a drop of a hat for the latest baron from Krygyzstan. But he is not a snob. He enjoys and is attracted to characters – especially driven ambitious men, off the beaten track, who have wealth and power. He can spot intelligence and drive, just as fast as he can identify a fine malt. Whisky is his passion, but it dovetails perfectly with the above.

Ken Loach
Director

Why this story?

Late last year, the number of unemployed young people in Britain reached over a million for the first time. We wanted to tell a story about this generation of young people, a lot of whom face an empty future. They can be pretty sure that they won't get a job, a permanent job, a secure job. Just what effect does that have on people and how do they see themselves?

You've made several films in Glasgow before. Why did you choose to set a film there again?

There are other cities like Liverpool and Newcastle or Manchester, or probably parts of the Midlands where you could find the same stories, but Paul's from the west coast so that's his idiom and that's where he writes best. And Glasgow's such a powerful location that it seemed the right place to set it – powerful in the culture of people there, in the sense of humour, the attitudes that people have to life, and the history that's produced there. It's a very collective, not an individualist culture, and yet people have as hard a time there as anywhere you could imagine.

Why a comedy?

Well just to be contradictory really. You always want to take an unexpected path. We made the film *Sweet Sixteen*, which was about lads, younger than these, but placed in an equally impossible situation, and that did end in tragedy. But the same characters will have incidents in their lives which are sometimes comic, and other times not. So we just thought we would pick one of the comic moments.

Is the process of making a comedy any different to making a serious piece?

No, the process is the same really, and I suppose the basic aesthetic is the same. Really, the comedy is usually the interaction of people, and the cracks they make, or the misunderstandings, or the time it takes for something to sink in… it's not slapstick. In a way it's a story with a few smiles in it rather than a comedy from start to finish – it certainly isn't that, because there are one or two quite dark moments in it. So the process is the same: it's about trying to release, or to enable people to go through the experiences, and if it's funny as it unfolds, well it's funny. If it's sharp or harsh then it should be that, and if it's unsympathetic then it's got to be that. The aim is just to have truthful interactions between people, and set them in a realistic framework. Then, if in real life they would make you smile, they make you smile; if in real life they'd make you cry, they make you cry, or make you angry or whatever.

Where did you start with *The Angels' Share*?

The biggest issue is always what's in the script and who are the characters. Then it's casting. We were looking for quite a long time and saw a lot of people for Robbie. It's just a gradual process of elimination. A lot of people are good but they're not good in exactly the way you want. The locations were just a question of spadework, so we saw a lot of distilleries – which was no hardship!

Describe Robbie

He's had a very harsh childhood, he's been involved in violence, he's served quite a long prison sentence in a young offenders' institution, and now he's really trying to get his life on track. He's bright and he's thoughtful, and he's met this girl who he is very fond of. They're having a child together. But from her parents' point of view, it's a disastrous relationship because all they see is a young thug and a young criminal, and the girl's father knows that world very well. He owns clubs, he's made a lot of money, he's moved to a better suburb, but he knows he's from the same mean streets that Robbie's from, so he knows that this lad has practically no chance of making a life for himself. Therefore, he's practically no chance of making a life for his daughter and their child either, so in the interests of his daughter he's going to use the methods of the street to keep them apart. You can have some sympathy for him, not with his tactics, but with the dilemma. If you've got a daughter and she's up with somebody who's probably involved in drugs, certainly involved in violence, no job, no way out – you know you'd be worried. Robbie's at that point where he's just going to struggle to be a father and to be a parent, to make some kind of living to support his family, which he sees no way of doing at the outset, and just sees no way out. Obviously the academic process passed him by because he was just being a teenage criminal from a world where that was the norm. So how do you get out of it? He says he's determined, but when that's your world and that's your perspective, it's very difficult to get out.

How do you decide when to cast established performers like Roger Allam in a role like Thaddeus?

It wasn't the fact that Roger was more established, it's just that I knew him and I knew he had a way of appearing sometimes; a way of appearing where you know he's up to something, but you don't know quite what. We met quite a lot of people as well, but nobody had that air that made you think there's something suspicious going on here but I'm not clever enough to work out what it is. And with a sense of humour as well. There's villainy, but it's villainy that makes you smile, and he has that absolutely, without having to articulate it.

What about the rest of the cast?

They're all fantastic. It was very good to work with William [Ruane] again – it's always good to have somebody in the cast who you can rely on. You know that you can often direct the others through that one person. I'd give William a note and he's professional enough to be able to include that in what he's doing. I know that'll draw a particular response from the others, without them being aware that they're being directed. Gary [Maitland], I don't think he's been doing any acting for a little while, but he's been in two of our films before, and he's just very… well he makes us smile. He has the air of living in parallel universe that operates with different laws to the rest of us. But also he has a very benign, good-humoured presence, and when disasters befall him you do feel for him as well. Jasmin [Riggins] was a delight: nice girl, very funny, but quite astringent and a good sharp presence.

The part we looked a long time for was finding a girl who would be Robbie's partner, Leonie. We thought it would be the easiest part but actually it turned out almost to be the hardest, because pitching the social level was very important. Because her father has made money they've moved out, so she's not mixing with the same group as Robbie and the others, and her father's tried to give her more of a middle-class background. But nevertheless she's close enough to Robbie's world to understand it. Finding someone who would just seem to fit was quite a challenge. There are different elements to balance: it can't be somebody posh, it can't be somebody too much from the street, but it should be someone that Robbie would feel was a real catch. We looked for a long time and Siobhan [Reilly] was someone we kept coming back to. She was lovely really, a smashing girl.

I should also say something about Charlie MacLean. Paul had written this character Rory and he'd met Charlie as a whisky expert so obviously Charlie was in his thoughts. He was going to be an advisor, and Paul said to me, 'You ought to meet him.' Once we'd met him, obviously he could just do it – it was inevitable that he would be in the film really. If somebody acted a character like that you'd get all the outward appearances of Charlie but it would be hard to have the knowledge and the actual concern, or the enjoyment of whisky that he obviously has.

How does whisky work as a metaphor in this film?

The moment you start talking about the whisky as a metaphor I'll get into pretentious areas! I think we've got to let the audience see that. The comparison is with *Kes*. In that film the bird, obviously, is the free spirit that the boy can never be, but we never talked about the metaphor at the time. The audience just has a sense of it.

How was the shoot?

There was an initial hiccup: I fell over. So there was a short delay. That was just an irritation. Apart from that the production team is so astute that they by and large troubleshoot the problems before we get to them. They are like a fine orchestra, with David Gilchrist, the first AD, leading the violins. They would probably manage without a conductor.

Is it more fun filming a comedy?

It's always just hard work really. You wake up in the morning in a cold sweat thinking, 'Am I going to get through the day? Are we going to get it done?' so I just find it's too much pressure for it to be fun. I mean there are funny things that happen in the course of the day invariably, but the overriding impression in the morning is just the work you've got to get through and the slight air of panic that you aren't going to make it. Part of the work of directing is hiding your internal panic, because you can't let it communicate.

Do you still have that after so many films?

Every day throughout the day, yes. Even days that seem quite easy there's still a sense of a mountain you've got to climb, and it doesn't seem to get any easier. Some things get easier in that you know whatever shortcuts there are to take, how you can manage it, but that's cancelled by just the physical effort of doing it. You've got to put energy into it; you can never be on the back foot, because if you are then everybody knows that and the energy levels sag. If the energy levels sag the performances will – you've got to generate the adrenalin for them to fire off. You can't have a totally placid set and expect people to give strong performances. And it's not fair to leave it to the performers: you can't just sit back and look at a monitor and say, 'Okay, off you go, do it.' They've got to have a sense of constructive pressure and constructive tension, and a constructive energy between people, because then they'll spark off each other. The director's got to generate that. It's all about what is going to be in front of the camera, what's in their eyes, what goes between them. So you've got to pace the little surges of energy and let there be a down period when you're setting up or moving or whatever and then wind it up again. It can be silly things like you've got to run about sometimes, just run about, and dash from them to the camera and around, and if somebody is showing a bit of energy, then it's contagious. It's why I think monitors are the death because when a director retreats behind a monitor, you're cutting yourself off instead of communicating. You're saying, 'Let somebody else do it.'

What did you know about whisky before this film?

Not a lot, and I don't know much now, except that I do know you have to sniff it more than taste it, which I like. The idea of really enjoying the nuances of a drink, yes there is something in that: that it isn't just something to throw down your neck and get obliterated, it's something to savour.

What do you hope the audience will take out of this film?
I hope they'll enjoy meeting the folks in it, particularly the young people who are either referred to as 'petty criminals' or 'benefit claimants' or whatever, and just see that they are rounded, humorous, proper, real people; and that for every one of that million unemployed statistic, there are a million kids who are facing a fairly hopeless future – and here's four of them. Aren't they interesting to meet and aren't they complex and valuable, worth something really? I hope they'll see that as well as enjoying the tale.

How does *The Angels' Share* sit among your previous work about young people?
The kids in previous films have had 'projects', like these four have the project of trying to raise money through their talent for nosing whisky. The lad in *Sweet Sixteen* had to raise money for a caravan for his mum. Billy Casper in *Kes* had to train the bird. They all show that idea of people who are generally disregarded having projects which they achieve or don't achieve, and enthusiasms and commitment and a talent which you don't know about. I suppose it's the old image of flowers on the bombsite: in the most unlikely surroundings, extraordinary things will happen. Young people are cast adrift into a world that, by and large, has no time for them. I wouldn't say there's nothing that a job wouldn't solve, but a proper secure craft, or skill, or job would solve most of the problems that these kids face, and that most people face. Because we are defined by our work, aren't we? Whether you're a craftsman in the building trade, a joiner, or plasterer or whatever, that's your identity and that's your sense of self. Well, now a lot of people don't have that. They are just what they're told they are which is 'benefit claimants' and constantly scrutinised in case they're cheating. What sense of self-worth can you have in that situation?

Rebecca O'Brien
Producer

We first talked about this film in some depth when we had an away day. I should point out that the Sixteen Films 'away day' was just Paul and Ken and I having a nice walk around Bath. The three of us got together and Paul was brimming with the characters that he'd thought of for this.

He wanted to go back to the world of *My Name is Joe*, *Sweet Sixteen* and *Ae Fond Kiss* – back to those people, to that world that he knows well. He wanted to take today's issues like youth unemployment and visit it within his favourite context. Rather than be didactic and bossy he's come up with a lovely little parable of the Angels' Share – which shows you there's a possible way of making things better somehow. It doesn't take a lot to improve things and I think that's what Paul's suggesting with the script.

Finance

We'd had such a good time with our French partners – Pascal Caucheteux from Why Not Productions and Vincent Maraval from Wild Bunch – on *Looking For Eric* that we kept working with them on *Route Irish*. And luckily for us we didn't put them off with that so they said, 'We'll do it again.' Those two companies have brought us a French co-production and a very good sales team. So it's very much the same financing structure as we did on *Looking For Eric:* we're still operating in the Cantona mode. It's all thanks to Eric – which is why Canto Bros are credited on the film.

We've put together a similar funding pattern as we've had in the past. That means a co-production with Italy, Belgium, UK and

France, with pre-sales to Spain and France and the UK and equity support from the BFI, France 2 and Studio Canal.

It's the usual patchwork quilt.

A lot of the money for our films comes from France. But that is out best territory so it makes economic sense for it to come from the people who appreciate our films most. For *The Angels' Share* the BFI came on board with a nice healthy investment. That really helped given we don't have a British broadcaster at this stage. We've got a strong UK pre-sale with Entertainment One, who also distribute the Twilight films. I have told them that I expect a premiere of similar magnitude to *Breaking Dawn* for *The Angels' Share*… Maybe we'll all turn out in tartan.

But they also did a very good job on *NEDS* last year which demonstrated how they could make what might normally be construed as a niche, arthouse film work – and work in Scotland in particular, where we hope *The Angels' Share* will find an audience.

Our funding partners are very generous now – they do recognise that we are grown up enough to make the films ourselves, so they don't interfere in the creative process. I must give the BFI the credit as well for really allowing us to be at arm's length. In the past when we've had equity funding, people have been desperate to get involved, but with Ken's experience it doesn't work – we'll just make the film we were going to make and that's the way we work. You know: old dog, new tricks.

To be frank, I think the less interference the better, with any filmmaker. You need to let them show their mettle, otherwise they just become a servicing engineer. Filmmakers need to be able to have the freedom to have ideas, so they can develop. Fortunately we do have that freedom but it shouldn't just be for us.

The Shoot

On day one of the shoot, a big day, Ken was very helpfully taking his dinner plate back to the caterers when he tripped on a step and bashed his head. It was a serious tumble, and we had to take a hiatus of three weeks. As we only take six weeks to shoot, that was a major hiccup. We had to put people on hold and ask cast and crew to be available for another three weeks. But mercifully everybody was up for it – there were no problems because everybody was dying to do it.

For the rest of the shoot, well, when you're making comedy it's always more fun. The weather in Scotland isn't always perfect. And it certainly wasn't always perfect: I remember we were filming up in a cemetery that overlooked Glasgow. It was a beautiful place but the weather was absolutely freezing – this was the middle of June and I was in a hat and gloves on top of a hill.

It was wonderful to go out beyond Glasgow, go to Edinburgh and the Highlands for filming. When you get out of an urban context and you end up filming in beautiful places in the middle of nowhere people are so happy to see you, to have a film happen. In those situations it's such a pleasure to make a film.

Michael Higson, our location manager, was working on the production for nine months, looking at distilleries. Fortunately he likes whisky. All the distilleries we worked at were so accommodating and helpful. Balblair is the setting for the last part of the film, the auction, Glengoyne is the exterior of the first distillery the group visits, and Deanston provides the interior. At Deanston there was a big storm a couple of nights before we were shooting there and they had a massive power cut. Their whole operation went down. They were just desperate to get it up and running so they could do it properly for us. They weren't so worried about their product!

For the auction we wanted something that was remote and looked remote, so that you could believe there's only one road south. We were also keen to have the pagoda roofs – we wanted it to be a picturesque setting representing all that is lovely about Scotland. It's like a dream location, a fantasy world, something one would only aspire to. So Michael looked at a lot of places and Balblair had that. I remember seeing its publicity photo. I felt, 'Yes, that's the one.' It's an hour's drive north of Inverness and there isn't a lot more beyond it: to the west of Balblair it's just mountains. But because it's on the east coast it doesn't have the fierceness of the Highlands, and the colours are lovely.

The three distilleries we chose are all independently run, a bit like independent film production companies, and there were lots of parallels in the way they work – so they recognised themselves in us. At Balblair, we discovered, their best market is France. We were a marriage made in heaven.

We had incredible support from lots of other whisky companies as well who gave us bottles to use in the film. We haven't been able to show nearly enough of their names so I apologise to them. They can at least know that the whisky has all gone to good causes. A bottle each to all of the cast and crew!

Robbie Ryan
Director of Photography

How did you first become involved?

I was cycling down the canal and I got a phone call from my London agent saying would I like to meet Ken Loach the next day. I met Rebecca and Ken at their offices and we had a nice chat. Twenty minutes later Rebecca rang and said do you want the job? I had to say yes. It was quite a whirlwind beginning.

What did you like about the script?

It's very well written. Paul Laverty is an amazing writer. It's a very different type of script to normal as it's not done in a typical style – because Ken and Paul work together all the time they've got a shorthand of how the scripts are, so there are a lot less scenes in the film than in most scripts, which I found quite intriguing. It's much more economical storytelling, made to be achievable in a small amount of time. Ken likes to work quickly. Paul's scripts enable him to do that. Most of all though, it was a really good read. There are great characters in the film. I love Scottish humour anyway. I'm a massive fan of films produced in Scotland because of the characters that come out of there. They're just crazy people. Reading the script I really wanted to help visualise those people because they're mental you know?

What were your initial thoughts on how you wanted the film to look?

I know Ken's work from years back. I knew that he would have a certain approach and that's what we talked about in the meeting

– how he would approach a scene and the whole process of how he works. In a way I felt that I would follow that style a bit. He has a way of working that you fit in to, not so much him fitting in to my way of working. It's been great to see a different style of filmmaking: Ken's approach is different to most filmmakers.

Was that a challenge?
It was a complete change. It was a different kind of film to the kind I would normally do. But to work with somebody like Ken is to learn a whole new process and I wanted to try that out, try a change of pace.

What was different?
Ken's photography is not a million miles away from mine. We're both really observational, but his observation is more from a distance whereas mine is as if I'm with the person. Walking and talking with them – that's the kind of camerawork I am maybe more known for. Ken's no different in as far as the observing and the details, it's just the camera is in a different place. He likes to be further away from the action, not to invade the space of the people in the film. The camera style I've become known for is much more as another character in the film.

Is the Scottish landscape a major part of the film?
Not really. Because you're following the story. That's a little bit of a rule that Ken has that cuts straight to the core of what he wants: he places people in among certain scenarios and it's really about how they react. You're concentrating on them and not so much on the location around them. Obviously it's a beautiful place: that goes without saying. But I think Ken's very focussed on the people in the piece, not so much the place.

What struck you about Ken Loach's directing?

Ken thinks about getting what he needs. If he gets it quickly and he's happy, he'll move on. If he thinks it takes a bit more time to get it he'll keep going until he gets it. And sometimes he's looking for accidents that might happen that he can capitalise on – he loves that. He just wants to open up the freedom to see what happens. That goes for everything in the way he produces it. The camera side of things isn't really to the fore, whereas on some films I've done, the visuals are very strong in order to tell the story. Ken doesn't want to draw too much attention to the visual style. He just wants to have you forget about it so you can really focus on what's happening with the story.

Most of the time he uses one camera because he loves being beside the camera. He gets a bit concerned if the other camera's over there and he can't see what it's doing. He likes standing beside the camera: he'd be telling me, 'try this, try that.' And I should add that that's great – nowadays digital filmmaking makes everybody sit in tents with black shades around them. Ken comes from a school of filmmaking where the director should be by the camera. Now, with digital, people can be directing from a hotel 300 miles away. That makes such a difference in terms of getting a performance. Whether the person in front of a camera is an actor or not an actor, they need to be told where to go and what to do by somebody. Is it going to be the cameraman or the director? I think it should be the director. Any time I've worked with directors who are close to the action and the camera there's a great energy about that. That's lost if you've got a person in another room.

What was the technical set-up on *The Angels' Share*?

Ken shoots on film, he edits on film – he's one of the few directors that do – and he loves that process. We used 35mm and we used Kodak stock, Arri cameras and prime lenses so very simple really. For this particular film it was a comfortable place to work from:

you know what you get, in terms of the look of it. From my point of view I like shooting on film. But it's an aesthetic choice really now. I can only fight as much as I can to say I prefer 35mm because technically I can't say digital is worse. But I definitely think I prefer the look of 35mm because of what the chemical process does to an image, as opposed to a digital process. That's personal preference – and I don't know how much longer I can hold out. In the low budget world where I come from you can't really fight the cost of digital versus 35mm. I think people like Steven Spielberg and Ken Loach will continue making films on film because that's where they've made their reputation. It's going to be a cause célèbre for people to try and fight and save it.

Fergus Clegg
Production Designer

The original plan was to film on Islay because that was where it was originally scripted. We went there and looked at all the distilleries but logistically it was too much – so within about two weeks of my starting on the film we realised it wasn't going to be Islay. And then we had to spend the next two weeks rushing around doing recces of mainland distilleries. Charlie MacLean was really helpful with locations and we also asked him to say whenever something wasn't right in the whisky realm.

The difficulty was you have this idealised view of how a distillery should be and you look at them and think, 'Aww, that's so quaint.' Then you get there and the mechanics aren't right. A lot of them have had the heart ripped out of them. Some of them are highly mechanised – at the big distillers they tend to industrialise the process. So you see a quite interesting building on the outside but get inside and it's a man in a glass room pushing buttons. That's not very romantic.

The process of making whisky is magical – how you turn this grain in to this very sought after drink. There's an amazing transformation that happens and the whisky industry trades on this. Originally Paul had written the script and it had a lot of those elements in it. We found that some of them were quite rare. The malting floors, for example, no longer exist by and large: it's all done somewhere else and then brought to the distillers. So elements of that heritage and tradition had already disappeared. We were looking for a mix of what's best visually and what's part of the process. It was almost impossible to find that in one place.

We started trying to find somewhere near Glasgow and then we radiated out further and further. We found Balblair distillery, where the climax of the film takes place, quite late on – it's almost as far north as you can go. It's fantastic, set in good countryside and with very, very helpful people.

When it came to the city setting, Ken's always keen to avoid the stereotypical approach. Harry's flat was difficult. He was someone who'd obviously had a major change in his life. His marriage had broken up, he'd lost his business and his livelihood and was starting afresh in a new town and a new place. But he's obviously a guy with a commitment to what he was doing in terms of helping turn these people's lives around. So we wanted somewhere that didn't look too affluent. The problem with shooting in these locations is the practicality of fitting a film unit in. The rooms have to be a certain size and the quality of the light is very important to Ken. He wants to use as much ambient light as possible so you look for large windows and a layout that works in terms of camera positions and shots through.

We looked at countless flats for Harry, but the good thing about Glasgow is a lot of those types of houses belong to Housing Associations so there is a believability in that. Although they look very grand they do actually house people from the right social group. To people from the south they might look disproportionately large and ornate but because of Glasgow's history and the tenement lifestyle they're actually correct.

For Robbie's flat it was a kind of squat type thing we were looking for and the one we found was in the Possilpark area. It has an amazing view over Glasgow and all these 1930s buildings. The area had such a bad reputation they're levelling it and starting again. So the property was almost entirely empty. It was supposed to be Robbie's friend's flat and Robbie has a room there. It was very basic, very pared down, no decoration, just scraps of carpet on the floor. Paul Brannigan, who plays Robbie, has been homeless so he knows it for real and he gave us a very clear brief. He came in one day and we said, 'What would you have in your room?' He said, 'Nothing.' There'd be a mattress, a pillow, a sheet over the window, and a black bag with some clothes in. The odd thing was he said he had a bit of cardboard under the bed he would use as an ironing board on the floor. So there was still that idea of caring for your appearance. It's probably the last thing you can control. Oh, and he said he'd had a weapon in the corner, a bit of metal or a machete, in case someone broke in.

Cast

Paul Brannigan
John Henshaw
Roger Allam
Gary Maitland
Jasmin Riggins
William Ruane
Siobhan Reilly
Charles MacLean

Paul Brannigan
Robbie

I had a job at a community centre when I first met Paul Laverty, the writer. I was working alongside Strathclyde Police on a project called the Community Initiative to Reduce Violence. Paul had heard about my past and my life story, but by that point a lot of people had because I'd been out there, been to youth centres, schools, doing football coaching.

The story I told them all was about growing up in Barrowfield in Glasgow: what I'd learned in my life about how drugs and alcohol can affect people, and the real facts about what it's like in prison. What it's like when you think you're in a gang and you think they're your friends and they say 'I'll back you up'. And they don't. How you can stay out of trouble through sport, through family. I tell them how I've got a wee boy now and how he's the most important thing that's happened to me.

Paul came and spoke to me and asked me to set up a meeting with myself and some boys that I'd been working with. We did that and then he asked me to go down and speak to Ken. But by this time I'd lost my job at the community centre. The way I'd lost that job was pretty bad. I felt as if I'd been stabbed in the back. I was gutted.

So when Paul asked me to go down and speak to Ken I felt what's the point? I'm fed up of telling my story and not getting anywhere. So I didn't go. Twice.

Then Paul phoned and basically gave me a kick up the backside. He said get your arse down here: this is a chance for you. Maybe not a big part but something. Because I had a wee boy and I was tired and it was just after Christmas I was feeling really, really low. 'Scuse my language but I basically went 'fuck it': at the time I was thinking if I get anything from this I can pay off one of my loans I took out for Christmas. So I went down and I just gave it everything I could possibly give.

I've never had any training as an actor so I just decided to go with my instinct, my feelings. Having so much experience through my life in every kind of situation you could possibly think of: that helped me. I tried to think of things in my past and use them – but not let it affect me in a way that I'm going to get obviously upset.

To be honest with you I realised that Ken was just a down to earth guy. He knows what he wants but he also gives you a chance to express your own opinions and feelings. As time went on through all the castings I just became myself – more confident and comfortable.

When I got the part I was more worried about meeting the crew and the rest of the cast, because of my background. To go into that environment not knowing what these people think of you is quite daunting. But within the space of about an hour I realised that they were the same as me – they just want to get on with the work, see everybody as equal. They've been so good to me – made me feel really comfortable.

Robbie has a real talent for whisky and so I've had a few tastings and I've picked up bits and bobs, especially about the smelling and the tasting. They gave me ten miniatures to take home for homework, some books and a notebook. I thought I was being daft. I was smelling and it smelt like wet dog, leather, seaweed, salt, peanuts – all different things. Then I would refer to the book and nine times out of ten some of the things I'd written were right.

So I started to take a wee interest. It was like a game. Now every time I'm in the pub I give it a go.

All in all it's worked out absolutely brilliantly for me. Usually any job I've been in – and in the last four years I've worked four or five different jobs – every day has been a struggle in the morning. With this I'm buzzing from the moment I get up.

It's been like therapy in a way. You think about the issues in the film and it reminds you how things were and what you've got now. It keeps your feet on the ground. For me that's the most important thing that could happen. If I get nothing out of this, fair enough. Just as long as I keep my feet on the ground, I'll be fine.

John Henshaw
Harry

Describe your character
I play Harry who's one of the supervisors on the community service that Robbie, Mo, Albert and Rhino are doing. He sort of gets on with them, sees something in them, so he decides to take them on a little day trip because a lot of them have never been out of Glasgow before. In this he incorporates a visit to a distillery and then the story goes from there.

Harry loves the old malt whisky and so he sets up this visit so they can appreciate a bit of their culture. Not to get them drinking, mind, but just to show you can have a nice civilised drop of whisky rather than getting out of your head on Stella or what have you. He wouldn't preach or try to educate them in that way – he just wants to show them another way.

We don't really know that much about Harry's background. He's divorced and he lives on his own. He's got a daughter but he's not seen his family for a bit. We just know that he's relocated from Manchester, he's up in Glasgow and he lives and works alone. He takes the kids to his heart. To say they're his family is a bit strong but they're all he's got really.

Why does he want to help them?
He forms a bond with Robbie because he's got something about him. I suppose he sees the way the girlfriend's father has

treated Robbie and he forms an attachment. He finds the whole gang funny – they're good kids. And he sees the good in them, considering where they are and what they've done. He just thinks they need to see a bit more of life, get out there, see what they can do. That's why he takes them for a day out on his own time. But then he becomes involved with Robbie's troubles to a certain extent when Leonie has the baby and Harry takes him to the hospital. He feels a little bit worried, because he knows that having a baby can be the start of a different life for Robbie – as long as Leonie's dad leaves him alone he can make a bit of a future for himself.

Is Harry a comic character?

Not specifically, but he does have that working-class humour if you like; the whole gang do. Glasgow is very much like Manchester, where I'm from. I always feel a great affinity with Glasgow and Glaswegians say the same. It's that dry, down to earth sense of humour they have. It's the way they deal with things. No matter where they are, the first thing they want to do is come up with a line about it. They're not necessarily telling jokes or being funny, it's just the way they are. Likewise, this film doesn't go out of its way to be a comedy, it's just the spirit of the people that are in it I suppose – no pun intended.

What struck you about the script?

Harry's looking after these kids who are doing community service for trifling things really. But they're not bad kids – all of them are likeable. I went out for a day with a community service team in Glasgow. We spent the morning outside a school scraping the railings and cleaning them off. They were good kids too. But they're trapped in an environment – Glasgow's a fantastic place but like anywhere else, some kids can't see the wood for the trees, they don't get the opportunity. Society's not geared that way now to get them on the ladder for employment – there are no apprenticeships or things like that. So what are the kids to do? Sometimes you just get took up the wrong path.

How does working with untrained actors compare to trained actors?

Well I'm not a trained actor so it depends on your definition of that! If you've got a script then it's a different story altogether but on Ken's films you don't get a full script so it's more about people thinking on their feet. A lot of trained actors don't like improvisation. Some are brilliant at it, some are not. Because of the really stringent casting process that Ken goes through he knows the people he's got before he starts. That's interesting when, for example, you say something to another cast member and you don't know what's coming back. So you react to it. It just creates a moment. People watching it sense that. That's the joy of it.

Your character is a whisky aficionado. Were you beforehand? Are you now?

I'm a real ale man, as you can probably tell from my physique. I didn't drink malt whisky, so I needed to get in to it for the part. I went to meet Charlie MacLean in Edinburgh who was fascinating, a really nice guy – he's the god of whisky and a character to boot. We spent the afternoon going through different whiskies from all sorts, teaching me the difference between the Highlands and the Lowlands, the peaty ones and stuff like that. Then we went to a couple of distilleries, and the science of it – the different types of whisky, smelling it, the legs – it was a real education for me. Since then I've got a couple of nice malts in the house and I've come to like it.

Roger Allam
Thaddeus

How did you come to be cast?
I'd worked with Ken and Rebecca before a few years back on *The Wind That Shakes The Barley* and they got in contact. No one knows what the full script is except them and they keep it secret but I was given the gist of who Thaddeus was, and I was free and delighted to do it.

Describe Thaddeus
He is a whisky dealer working somewhere in the grey area of criminality, really. He deals in very, very expensive whisky for very rich collectors and clients who have spare millions hanging about and want to spend it. He provides them with rare things. I imagine he comes from a posh background but he isn't especially rich himself.

What is Thaddeus's relationship with Robbie?
He first meets Robbie at this tasting in Edinburgh and he spots someone who's got a very good nose. Robbie can judge whisky and he's got an instinct and knowledge beyond his years. One of the things about Thaddeus is that he's essentially democratic. He doesn't care about people's class, background or where they come from or who they are – I mean when it comes to his clients he's probably dealing with the Russian mafia for God's sake! So if someone's got a skill or a talent and he sees a spark in them, which

he does with Robbie, he's perfectly prepared to use it. Whatever it takes to get the whisky he's after.

Does working without a complete script require a change of style?

You don't need to know everything to be able to play a scene. You just need enough to go on. If I think about who I, Roger Allam, am, everything I can remember I can recall – but I don't remember it all the time. You don't carry the knowledge of who you are around with you all the time, at the forefront of your consciousness. It's like that in acting – you just need to have an idea of the type of person you are playing. The advantage to Ken's method is you can get stuff made with a greater amount of freedom. In terms of acting, the great John Gielgud said that, 'Style is knowing what play you are in.' As an actor you work within the guidelines and perimeters laid down by the people that you're working with.

How was filming in Scotland?

I've been very lucky. Most of the days I did were absolutely glorious, so I experienced none of the hardship that all of the rest did, in terms of the weather, which I gather was Antarctic at times. I hadn't filmed in that particular bit of Scotland before but when I was a child my parents used to bring the family on walking holidays to the Highlands, and I've filmed in Scotland several times – *The Queen* was shot around various places in the Highlands and the Lowlands, standing in for Balmoral. So yes, I know it and it was lovely to be up there.

This is your second time working with Ken Loach. How does it compare to other productions?

It's hugely enjoyable, because it's relaxed and it tends not to be overshot. If you shoot things from loads of different angles with loads of different lenses you can make a magnificent film, but in terms of acting the task then is to try to keep it fresh for every take. That can become very wearisome. Whereas on something like this you tend to do less of that and things therefore are fresher and more immediate. It's not casual – though it feels like that in a way. I suppose it's because he's shooting in a way that is more like how the human eye sees. Rather than suddenly going in to a dramatic close-up or shooting from a very arty angle, it's more like how you would see it as a human being.

As an actor with plenty of experience how do you find working with actors with no experience?

Well I do remember that on *The Wind That Shakes The Barley* there was a particular gag in a scene that a very, very sweet old man playing this part couldn't do – because he didn't have the technical facility to do it. So it's swings and roundabouts. While you gain in terms of a freshness and looseness you can sometimes have to cut your losses. I guess also that young people, because there's an awful lot of reality television, they're more used to the notion of being filmed. When I first made a film, when I came from the theatre, the whole process of being filmed was very strange. Being in the theatre seemed much more real to me. Whereas for youngsters now they're much more at home in the business of there being a camera watching what you're doing.

What was your whisky knowledge before this film?

I used to drink whisky but what I discovered over many years was that it didn't go terribly well with red wine. And I have rediscovered that in the course of making this film! As I say, I used to drink whisky and enjoy it; I don't drink it very much now. But I had a wonderful session with Charlie MacLean who's injected a certain amount of knowledge into me, so I have enough to go on as Thaddeus.

Gary Maitland

Albert

How did you come to be cast?

What happened was I've done a couple of films with Ken before – I was in *Sweet Sixteen* and *Tickets*. He must have remembered me so he gave us a wee call and asked us to come in for a chat. I went in and he told us the basics about the film – not too much, just a bit. He asked me if I wanted to do it and obviously I did, but I've actually got a job – I work for street cleansing for the council – so I had to take seven weeks' unpaid leave.

Describe Albert

Albert brings a wee bit of comedy to the film. He just does crazy things. He's one of the lads, likes drinking but he also comes out with some stuff in the film that you wouldn't expect him to say. He's there for the comedy but there's some dialogue in it that's a wee bit serious, you might say a bit more profound, too.

Does his background have any parallels with your own?

I live in Castlemilk and I work in Cambuslang area so I'm local. And I like getting a laugh from my own friends like he does – I like being a wee bit of a joker, know what I mean? And he likes Buckfast [fortified tonic wine] so I can relate to that – I used to drink Buckfast myself in the past! To be honest I didn't know a lot about whisky beforehand but I've definitely improved my knowledge. But I'm still more in to Buckfast.

How was the shoot?

It was great being with the group. Paul's [Brannigan] cool. I think he's done a cracking job, especially as it's the first time he's done stuff. We've all been staying on a local caravan site and had a bit of time together, playing darts and having a few drinks – just chilling. I like that you don't know what you're going to be doing when you come in each day because they don't show you the whole of the script. Ken gives you lines – he tells you to just sneak that one in and the other actors don't know what's going to happen so you get an instant reaction from them. To be honest I've never experienced anything else other than Ken's films. I know what Ken's like, I know how he works and I'm sure that's one reason why they've got me back. But I'm looking forward to getting back to my work because I enjoy it too.

What would you say *The Angels' Share* is about?

I would say it's about a young boy who's got a rough background. He's trying to make a better life for himself through whisky. Hopefully things will work out for him.

Jasmin Riggins
Mo

How did you come to be cast?

I was cast through an agency and I went through five or six auditions before I got the part. It was improvising with six or seven different people doing different things in different situations, but I never had a clue who I was playing or what the story would be. Actually that was quite exciting because you're anxious to know about everything. The day I found out I was cast was the day that they told me and the rest of the cast something about who we were playing. It was the same day I was meant to be going to another audition so it only sunk in a few days later.

Describe your character

She's got attitude and she doesn't really care what people think, and she doesn't take any crap. It's really good fun to play!

Were you aware in the beginning that Mo and the gang were such important parts?

No! I didn't actually realise until a good way in to the shoot what the film is really heading towards because, as you know, we aren't shown future scripts so we don't have a clue. It's only in the last few weeks of the shoot that I thought, 'God, so this is what I'm going to be doing.' I didn't actually realise how close we were going to be, me and Gary and Will and Paul – and how important we were in the film. I didn't really think it was such an important part as what it has been so it's been great to realise that. It's brilliant that we're at the centre of the film. I love working with them – it's just like four boys. I'm not a tomboy but I can mix it with the boys if that makes sense. I've always had friends who were boys at school, older boys too, so I'm used to it.

Are there any parallels between you and Mo?
Well I've not got red hair for starters. But I suppose I have got a bit of attitude. Obviously I am playing her but there's some things that are similar – maybe I wouldnae take any crap off some people. I'd stand up for myself, put it that way. Plus I'm from Glasgow and we get to speak like we normally do for once. Although of course I don't want people to think that's the only way I can speak because I'm swearing every second word that comes out of my mouth. People will think I've got a foul mouth, but I don't swear like that. Well, not as much.

Have you acted before?
I used to do dancing – I've done dancing for years. Then I faded away from it but I did drama at school and so mum put me in to drama classes. That's when I thought I would quite like to do more of this. This is the biggest thing that I've done – I'm 18 – and it's been amazing, brilliant.

William Ruane
Rhino

Describe your character

He's just a wee bit of a jack the lad. A sarcastic type – likes a joke, likes a laugh, just gets on with everybody and he's game for anything. One thing though: I still haven't worked out why he's called Rhino. Maybe because he's thick-skinned. Or always horny. Anyway, his story is he's up in court for riding and humping and putting cones on statues. And he gives some cop grief, aye, which was fun.

How did you come to be cast?

This is the fourth time I've worked with Ken – I was in *Sweet Sixteen*, *Tickets*, and I had a role in *The Wind That Shakes The Barley*. I just got a call to meet up for a coffee and a chat. He told us about the project. They called me back for another coffee and told me that they wanted me to play a role. But they didn't know which one yet. Then obviously the part of Rhino came up and it was great to be back. They asked me to come along and help with the casting as well. We were constantly casting, doing scenes among ourselves and getting that vibe between one another.

Are there any parallels between you and Rhino?

As far as community service and going to jail goes? Nah, I'm a good boy when it comes to that. I love a laugh as well and I'm up for anything. But I'm not a Buckfast fan – it's a horrible wine that the young 'uns drink. So on drink I'm the opposite of Rhino. Mind you I'm not much of a whisky man either. I just don't like the taste. I've never been in a distillery before but now I've had the full tour and I know a lot about how whisky is made. So you learn a lot. I made sure I had a wee sip at the wrap party.

How was the shoot?
The shoot was great. When you've worked with Ken before you know what to expect – which is not a lot! You don't get told much. We only know what's happening right in front of us because that's the way Ken goes. But it was good to be back and do the full duration of the shoot again. The last time I got a full six weeks was on *Sweet Sixteen*. Of course, there were a few surprises along the way. There was a scene when we were hitch-hiking in the back of a trailer, and there were a couple of furry animals in the back – and Ken hadn't told us until the last moment. It was sheep at first, then it was a couple of shaggy dogs eventually. They got a bit rowdy – me and Gary [Maitland] were sitting in the back of this trailer, bobbing along and they got a bit playful: one was growling, trying to bite our feet off. Just goes to show: you can't choose your co-stars.

Siobhan Reilly
Leonie

Describe Leonie?

She's a really interesting character. She's a girl who is from a very hardworking family and was brought up with good manners and good ethics in life. But her father was obviously not brought up in the same way she was. He's had a harder childhood living in not such a well off area. He brought her up to try and do better for herself in life. Then she got involved with a boy, Robbie, who's from a similar background to her father – and obviously this hasn't gone down very well with the family.

But she's the sort of person who judges someone for who they are. She's not looking at their situation. In Robbie she saw a good person who's not had a good chance in his life. At the beginning of the film they have a child. For them it becomes such a bonding thing. It becomes their chance to grow together with their child and show people that they are a loving family, show that they can do it their way and they don't need other people around them to make that work. It's just a question of whether or not circumstances will let them.

How did you come to be cast?

I was working as a supply teacher although I have been an actor before. My boyfriend had noticed a posting on a website saying that Ken was looking for someone so I got in contact and went in. You could tell that he was really interested in getting to know you as a person first of all and it was all quite playful so you felt really comfortable and at ease. You could see he just wanted to draw out different aspects of your personality. I met them several times with different actors just trying to find that chemistry. I met Paul [Brannigan] a few times and tried different things out just to see whether we gelled together. It meant we had a good relationship for when the filming started.

Did you have any inkling of the character you'd be playing?
I had no idea what I was going for, not a clue. Even halfway through the casting process I still had no idea what the role would be. I don't think Ken really knows when he first meets you what your role will be either. He was trying to suss out where I might fit in. It means when you get cast it's a bit of a leap of faith because you don't know what your journey's going to be after that. You just have to trust and hope that all goes well.

Is Leonie's social situation one that's familiar to you?
Very familiar. I'm from Petersburn in Airdrie, which is a little town on the outskirts of Glasgow. I trained as an actor when I was younger and I also trained as a teacher.

All of the filming was done in places I live near or know. I come from a very working-class family and in my teaching work I deal with a lot of young parents and single parents and a lot of poverty as well. I like the fact that this film shows how people are people no matter where they come from, in spite of things not being the greatest for them. Where I live, there's not a lot of money or opportunities for people but they're good hearted people who would do anything for you. You see that in the film.

Can you have a comedy when such serious issues are at stake?
The film shows how for all people do have hardships in life people have also got a sense of humour and a sense of fun about them.

And that gets them through situations as well. Friendships and relationships make you who you are, for all you may have troubles.

How did your and Paul's relationship evolve?

When we met we just got on. You know how sometimes you meet somebody and you just click? I think we understand each other – Paul and I have got very similar backgrounds, so we both understood where these characters were coming from. Paul was quite a young parent as well – he's got a little child; he understands the social implications of that. And I know a lot of people in Paul's situation. It just seemed to gel really well from the start.

What surprised you once filming began?

Up until filming I knew my back story but I didn't really know what was going to happen next. On the very first day we went to meet the costume people and the head costumer said, 'I need to ask you questions about your sizes. But I can only ask you what shoe size are you?' I had a sneaky suspicion there might be a baby involved but I didn't know that at the time. It turns out they didn't ask me for clothing sizes because I was going to be in maternity wear! I hadn't known I was going to be pregnant in the film! When I found out I said I had two sisters who'd had babies recently, so I could bring in lots of maternity wear. They asked if I could bring in a baby! So then my nephew got involved and he is the baby you see in the film.

Charles MacLean
Rory McAllister

Describe you character

Essentially I just play me – a whisky expert called Rory McAllister. He hosts a tasting in Edinburgh and is asked to provide the provenance of the 'Holy Grail' whisky. This is my acting debut. Well, the last time I acted on stage was at school in Marlowe's *Faustus*. I was very flattered to be asked. But thank God Ken doesn't operate with scripts – I couldn't have done it with a script. Whereas ad-libbing wasn't too much of a problem.

You are a Master of the Quaich. What is that?

There's a whisky industry organisation called The Keepers of the Quaich, which was invented in the late eighties to honour those who had done good service to Scotland and the Scotch whisky industry. I became a Keeper in 1992. They have a further rank called Master and there are only 50 of them. I became one in October 2009.

What does the job involve?

Nothing at all. Except occasional dinners at Blair Castle, which is the society's HQ.

Where does your expertise in whisky come from?

Practice. I started writing about whisky in 1981 for various whisky companies. I did formal training in sensory evaluation with the Scotch Whisky Research Institute in 1992, I published my first book that year and it was really after that that my career swerved off towards whisky.

How did you become involved in *The Angels' Share*?

I got a call out of the blue in January 2010 saying we're making a film that might feature whisky quite strongly. The scriptwriter will be in Scotland next week and he'd like to speak to you. Paul Laverty phoned up and I said come along whenever – but make it after six o'clock. Then we can have a few drams and I can bore for Scotland on the subject.

Quite frankly I get contacted by production companies about once a year and nothing ever comes of it, so I didn't take it that seriously. Paul Laverty is an extremely modest chap so it was only about 40 minutes into the conversation that he mentioned that the director was to be Ken Loach. I immediately stood up and paid attention.

Over the course of a year we spoke about locations and contacts and then the script arrived in February 2011 and I was one of the very few people to see the whole of it. Again, I gave them my ha'penny-worth in relation to whisky.

I'm a consultant at Bonhams, the auctioneers, and they were doing an auction of a single bottle of whisky in late February. It was a 70-year-old Glenlivet that was to be auctioned for the Japanese Tsunami fund. They asked me to say a few words to set up the provenance of this bottle before it was auctioned off. I phoned Rebecca [O'Brien, Producer] and said single lot auctions are not that common: if it would be of any use for you and Ken to see this you should come.

It happened that Ken was in Glasgow at the time so they came. The following day Rebecca phoned up and said 'Would you like the role of Rory?' I said, 'I'm not an actor.' She said, 'Well that's the point. You just have to play yourself.' And so that's how I got landed in this part.

What was tweaked in the script at your suggestion?
The main tweak was the 'Holy Grail' whisky itself. It was originally envisaged to be a Port Ellen. That's a closed distillery on Islay and is highly collectable but it is released every year. They wanted to make a really big price for the auction in the film so I suggested Malt Mill. Malt Mill was a distillery that was built within the Lagavulin distillery on Islay in 1908 and operated until 1962. There is no known Malt Mill around. There are three claimant bottles but it's generally reckoned that two of them are fakes so it's extremely rare. Whisky collectors around the world – of which there are many nowadays – would give their eye teeth for a bottle of Malt Mill, let alone a small cask of Malt Mill, which is what's on offer in the film.

Otherwise I didn't change anything significant – really just the language. Paul would refer to the 'dunnage' – when it should be a 'dunnage warehouse'. Just little things like that. Only whisky experts would know the difference.

Do auctions like the one in the film actually happen?
Collecting whisky is becoming more and more popular. The biggest collections are in Italy but there are collections all over the world. Some people specialise in individual distilleries, Lowland malts, pre-1920s malts. There's also a thriving market in forgeries now because of this interest. So an auction just as this one would attract considerable interest.

How did you go about educating the cast?
We did two days with John [Henshaw] and Roger [Allam]. They didn't need much educating really. They took to it like ducks to water. I was hugely impressed with their noses. I taught them what

they would be expected to know to help them get in to character. These fellows would probably know a bit of the history, they would know how to handle a whisky glass and how to nose and taste. They would also know about prices and the industry today. With John we went straight to Glenkinchie distillery just outside Edinburgh so he could see what a distillery looks like. Then we went back in to town and had some lunch in a restaurant that has an excellent collection of old whiskies. Then we went to my place outside Edinburgh and had a substantial nosing and tasting. With Roger I think we went straight in to the nosing and tasting.

Could a boy from the tenements in Glasgow like Robbie genuinely have a naturally brilliant palate?

The truth of the matter is that we're all similarly equipped. There is a phenomenon called specific anosmia that is like odour blindness where you cannot detect certain groups of smells but by and large we all have the same tools. With a bit of practice and concentration we can all do it. The work is mainly done with the nose, as, compared to our mouths, our noses are infinitely more sensitive. To identify a smell and then to name it just takes practice. Robbie's interest first of all develops with Harry. Then he starts reading books. That's how it would work – interest followed by practice, nosing, tasting, discussing, taking notes and working at it. It's perfectly credible.

What's your favourite whisky?

The one that you're about to buy me! To be honest most of my work is done with malt whisky so at six o'clock in the evening when I reach for a dram it would be a blend that I'm looking for. And probably my favourite blended scotch is Johnnie Walker Black Label. Simple as that.

A Lesson in the Appreciation of Malt Whisky

Charles MacLean
[aka Rory McAllister]

> *'The notion that we can possibly develop a palate for whisky is guaranteed to produce a smile of derision in any company except that of a few Scottish lairds, farmers, gamekeepers and bailies, relics of a vanished age of gold when the vintages of the north had their students and lovers.'*
>
> Aeneas Macdonald, *Scotch Whisky*, 1930

Note the date of the above quotation. 1930. How times have changed – and changed for the better! The whole world now acknowledges what sublime drinks 'the vintages of the north' – single malt Scotch whiskies – are, and over the past twenty-odd years more and more have been made available by their makers for our delectation.

I am often asked: 'What is the correct way to drink whisky?'

The answer is that there is no *correct* way to drink; you should *enjoy* it as you like. Our grandfathers drank it with ice and soda (now becoming popular again in Japan, I'm told). Until recently – particularly in Glasgow and on the West Coast – lemonade was popular, known affectionately as 'ginge' (i.e. 'ginger'), and available free in bars. In China today they favour mixing with sweet green tea. In Spain with Coca-Cola; in North America with Canadian Dry Ginger Ale; in Brazil with coconut water… It really doesn't matter: Enjoy *Scotch* as you like.

By 'Scotch' all these markets think 'blended Scotch'. Malt

whisky is a different creature altogether, worthy of appreciation on its own and not to be 'covered' by mixers. Nor is it a drink to be rushed; it rewards consideration. After all, its creation is a work of high craft – of alchemy even – and most malts have been matured for 10, 12, 15 or more years.

Appreciation

'Appreciation' is more than just 'drinking'; more even than simple 'enjoyment'. If you like it is 'enhanced enjoyment'. It stimulates the brain cells, encourages conversation as well as contemplation. It is best done in company (so you can compare notes), but is also rewarding in isolation.

Here are a couple of tips – passed on by me to John Henshaw (Harry), and by him to Paul Brannigan (Robbie).

First, to appreciate malt whisky to the full, you use your nose as much as your palate; you savour aroma as well as taste. Never forget that 'flavour' is, by definition, a combination of the two.

As a result, an appropriate glass is essential – one with a bowl, so you can swirl the liquid, and a rim that narrows slightly so as to direct the aroma up your nose. In the trade we use a 'spirits nosing glass', but an ISO (the European standard white wine glass) is fine. Even a Paris goblet red wine glass is better than the tumbler which whisky is typically served in. These are fine for enjoying Scotch with ice and a mixer, but hopeless for appreciating malt whisky.

Next tip: don't add ice, since this closes down the aroma. Malt whisky is best enjoyed at a chilly 'room temperature', around 15°C.

On the other hand: do add a little still water, since this both opens up the aroma and makes the spirit easier to taste. I like tap water – it is fresher than bottled water – but do smell and taste it first to make sure it has no taint of chlorine. If you are using bottled water, go for Scottish waters like Highland Spring: they tend to be soft, while French or Italian waters tend to be 'mineral rich' and hard.

Procedure

Having found an appropriate glass, pour a decent measure of whisky, leaving plenty of room to swirl it. Spin the liquid in the glass and consider its 'appearance': its colour (various shades of gold and amber), its texture (indicated by the 'legs' which trickle down once you have swirled – slow and thick legs indicate a big body; thin and fast trickles suggest a light body) and when, later, you add water, its clarity (a slight haze indicates that the whisky has not been chill-filtered – a good sign).

Now take a sniff. You may well find it slightly prickly on the nose. Take a small sip to assess key characteristics. Then add just enough water to take away any nose-prickle – possibly only a teaspoon, typically half as much as the measure you have poured. Whisky blenders habitually assess samples as 20% Alcohol By Volume (ABV), but you may find this a bit low.

Swirl and nose again. Now take a mouthful – enough to coat your tongue. Squish it about so your palate is well covered – some people like to breath in through their mouths while they're doing this (a trick learned from the wine trade). Concentrate a) on the liquid's texture, its 'mouth-feel': soft, smooth, viscous, acerbic, tannic, drying are common descriptors, b) on what 'primary tastes' you can detect and how they balance each other, c) its overall taste, d) its finish (short, medium or long) and e) its aftertaste (if any).

There are four primary tastes – sweet, sour/acidic, salty, bitter/dry. Sweetness is detected principally on the front of the tongue, acidity and saltiness at the sides and dryness towards the back, as you swallow. Now take another sip and see whether the taste reminds you of anything, note the finish (short, medium or long) and ask yourself whether there is any aftertaste.

It's all common sense really, but following this simple procedure will certainly enhance your appreciation, and thus your enjoyment, of the dram in your glass.

Sensory Evaluation

I have said that flavour is by definition a combination of smell and taste – so it is wrong to talk only of 'whisky tasting' when we're engaged in evaluating the flavour of a whisky. In truth, as will be clear from the above, we are using all our senses, which is why the procedure is properly termed 'sensory evaluation':

Sight	– To consider colour, texture, clarity
Smell	– To gather data, trigger memories and associations, assess complexity
Touch	– The 'nose-feel' and 'mouth-feel' effects referred to
Taste	– The primary tastes, overall taste, finish and aftertaste
Sound	– Perhaps we don't use this sense, except to enjoy the sound of a new bottle being opened and poured!

Of all our senses, smell is the most important for the whisky assessor – which is why such individuals are called 'noses' in the whisky trade. Blenders and quality control assessors obtain all the information they require by smell alone.

What is smell and how do we detect odours?

This is a surprisingly thorny topic – smell is the least understood of our senses – and too big a subject for this lesson. Suffice to say that scents are carried by volatile odour-bearing molecules called 'congeners' and are detected by a small mucous-covered pad behind our noses called the olfactory epithelium.

From this little pad, olfactory nerves plug directly into the base of our brains, into a region called the limbic system – the most primitive part of our consciousness, formed before we humans even became mammals: formed when we were still reptiles.

Furthermore, this ancient part of our brain is also the seat of memory and emotion – which is why smells are so evocative and can be so moving. As Lyall Watson writes in *Jacobson's Organ* (1999):

> '*Smell is our most seductive and provocative sense, invading every domain of our lives, providing the single most powerful link to our distant origins… But it is also mute, almost unspeakable, defying description and collection, challenging the imagination.*'

And Diane Ackerman in *A Natural History of the Senses* (1990):

> '*Nothing is more memorable than smell… Smells detonate softly in our memory like poignant landmines hidden under the weedy mass of the years. Hit a trip-wire of smell and memories explode all at once. A complex vision leaps out of the undergrowth.*'

The Silent Sense

But if smell is 'mute', how do we describe what we smell in a glass of whisky?

The language we use is dependent on:

a) who we are addressing (colleagues, customers, friends, the general public…)

b) the purpose of our communication (to analyse, to sell, to entertain, for fun…)

This gives rise to two broad approaches to sensory evaluation: the objective or analytical approach and the subjective or hedonic approach (as in 'hedonism' – the pursuit of pleasure).

The first approach is used by whisky blenders and quality assessors and is addressed to colleagues in the same company, not to consumers. Their approach is scientific and analytical; they seek to be as objective as possible, and to suppress all subjective, personal impressions and emotions.

Their words do not necessarily even have to be comprehensible to outsiders – although it is essential that each assessor knows

233

exactly what they mean when they use a particular descriptor, and for this reason the language they use is strictly prescribed.

For example, the quality experts at Diageo, the world's largest whisky company, use a vocabulary of only fourteen words to assess every batch of new make spirit from all the company's twenty-eight malt distilleries, each of which is required to produce spirit with a specified character. Samples are nosed blind and the assessors apply simple words to each one – such as 'grassy', 'meaty', 'nutty', 'spicy', 'waxy'… Woe betide the distillery manager if his spirit is judged as 'grassy' when it should be 'fruity'!

Some companies go even further, using language derived from chemistry. Here is a list of 'Standard Reference Odours in New-make Grain Spirit' used by another company:

Name	Description
Acrolein	sharp, acidic, pungent
B	meaty, Marmite, burnt rubber
DMTS	cooked cabbage, drains, spent matches
Feints	amyl alcohol, plastic, cheese
Acetal	green apples
Di-acetal	buttery, sweet, heavy
Ribes	cats, tomato leaves, redcurrant leaves
Phenols	iodine, carbolic, peat smoke, bonfires

Accurate and objective descriptors, but of use only in-house.

Subjective Assessment

Our approach as consumers or guides to consumers (my job!) is far more subjective. We are not limiting ourselves to the strict scientific constraint of objective description. We can open our minds, draw upon our own life's experience, say whatever we like – nothing is set in stone, and there are no pejoratives when describing whisky!

Clearly, this applies especially when you are talking with friends or sitting on a private nosing panel. If your subjective notes are to be relayed to others or used for specific purposes – not least to sell the whisky – a degree of objectivity is required: your descriptors must be as accurate as you can make them, and they must also be understandable to your audience – there is no point in identifying 'After Eight' aromas to an audience unfamiliar with such chocolates!

We are free to use figurative language which appeals directly to the senses, sometimes in a surprising way. The imagery we use may be as personal as you like – 'smells like my grandfather's pyjamas' – and communicates by allusion not fact – nobody but you has smelled your grandpa's PJs, but everyone can imagine the smell of such…!

Often similes and metaphors are used.

Similes liken one sensation to another and are often prefixed by 'it reminds me of…', or simply 'like…': 'this whisky reminds me of a distant bonfire on a beach', 'smells like wet sheep', 'like a jelly baby in a cement mixer'.

Metaphors describe the sensation in terms of something it resembles: 'a plate of freshly cut apples and pears', 'summer rain on dry ground', 'the fugitive aromas of the earth itself'.

Sometimes abstract terms are useful – particularly when you are struggling to identify a precise aroma and need to buy time! Such words are imprecise and merely indicate a characteristic. Common examples in relation to whisky are 'smooth', 'clean', 'fresh', 'coarse', 'rich', 'young', etc., and each of these give rise to its 'contrasting pair': 'rough', 'grubby', 'stale', 'refined', 'thin', 'old'.

Flavour Wheels

In the late 1970s an attempt was made to make the language of whisky evaluation more disciplined and systematic. The research institute given this task published their results in the form of a wheel – a device already used by the wine and beer trades. The 'hub' of the wheel identifies a number of 'cardinal aromatic groups' – a simple wheel has six segments: 'malty', 'fragrant', 'fruity', 'peaty', 'pungent' and 'woody'.

The next two tiers expand upon this (see Flavour Wheel on page 238), the third offering suggestions for the kind of subjective descriptors which might come to mind at a nosing. They are suggestions only! There are an infinite number of odours, and we can't possibly map them all. Sensory chemists have managed to identify 300 odours in samples of malt whisky, and estimate there may be as many again still to be isolated and named!

For me, the value of a Flavour Wheel is as a quick checklist to run through and focus the mind while you are addressing the difficult task of identifying what you smell. Often the 'spokes' of the wheel are graduated, so you can also measure the intensity of each aroma on a scale of, say, one to ten.

Imagination

I repeat: smells have an objective origin, deriving from chemical compounds, the 'congeners' I have referred to. But, as Diane Ackerley (quoted above) says, they 'detonate softly in the memory', bringing to mind past experiences – both real and imaginary – which all add to our appreciation and enjoyment of the whisky in the glass.

Scotch malt whisky is acknowledged to be the most complex of all spirits, but there is more to it even than this. As one of my mentors puts it: 'when you buy a bottle of whisky, you are buying a hell of a lot more than "liquor in a bottle"; you are buying craft and time, history and tradition'.

To put it another way, if I might be so immodest as to quote from the introduction to my book, *Malt Whisky* (1997):

'Scotland is at the heart of the matter, for malt whisky is the quintessence of Scotland. It recollects the land of its birth with every sip — peat hags and bog myrtle, the sun on the loch, the rain on the mountain, white beaches and salt spray: the fugitive aromas of the land itself. It also speaks of the people of Scotland — the tough farmers who developed the art of distillation, the intrepid smugglers who kept the still-fires burning in the face of the law, the remarkable entrepreneurs who built a world market for Scotch in the later decades of the nineteenth century.

'And in its effects, malt whisky epitomises the inherent dichotomy of the Scottish psyche — at once passionate and rational, romantic and ironic, mystical and sceptical, heroic and craven, full of laughter and despair.'

Ken Loach and Paul Laverty's genius is to have expressed so much of this in *The Angels' Share*. I am honoured to have contributed my small contribution to this charming film!

A SIMPLE FLAVOUR WHEEL

Tier 1	Tier 2	Tier 3
Malty	Cereal	Weetabix, bran flakes, Rice Krispies, Horlicks, malt barn, Marmite, pot ale
	Green	green sticks, cut grass, green veg, apple mint, green tomatoes, pine
Fragrant	Fresh fruit	bananas, peaches, figs, pears, apples, raspberries, cherries, strawberries
	Floral	scented, perfumed, rose, coconut, gorse, lavender
	Solvent	bubblegum, fresh paint, acetone, cellophane, pine essence
Fruity	Dried fruit	raisins, sultanas, dried figs, mince pies, Xmas cake, marmalade
	Honey	mead, heather-honey, runny-honey, beeswax, clover flowers
	Vanilla	toffee, fudge, treacle, crème brûlée, custard, caramel
Peaty	Smoky	moss, fresh peat, barbeque, bonfire, coal fire hearth, Lapsang Suchong tea, kippers, smoked cheese, smoked ham
	Medicinal	TCP, iodine, creosote, coal tar, Germoline, hospital corridors
Pungent	Sulphury	starch, pencil eraser, burnt rubber, exhaust fumes, spent matches, fireworks
	Meaty	gravy, roast meat, pork sausages, leather, shoe polish, cheese, hide
	Vegetative	drains, marsh gas, brackish, bogs, cabbage water, stale tobacco
Woody	Winey	sherry, chardonnay, port, madeira, brandy
	Oily	cream, butter, candlewax, chocolate, olives, almonds, hazelnuts, linseed oil
	Wood	oak, saw-dust, musty, coffee grounds, cigar boxes, burnt cake, ginger, sap

Tasting Notes

As I mentioned earlier, the language of whisky is not prescribed; you can say what you like, reach deep into a personal vocabulary (although maybe nobody will understand you!), employ outlandish metaphors with gay abandon, allow yourself to be transported back to childhood scents from sweetie shop, bonfire night, behind the bicycle shed...

Here are a few examples. You will see that I have organised my comments in the order in which I suggest you look at, nose and taste the whisky.

First, a straightforward impression of the standard Deanston bottling at 12 years old:

DEANSTON
12YO Highland Single Malt Whisky @46.3%

Deanston operated as a cotton mill for nearly 200 years (1785–1965), before being converted into a distillery in 1969. The substantial buildings were designed by Richard Arkwright, one of the towering giants of the Industrial Revolution, and the inventor of the carding and spinning machines which made the mass production cotton yarn possible.

The 12YO is bright gold in colour. Fleetingly, the first aroma reminded me of Fry's Orange Cream chocolate bars. This was soon eclipsed by sweet shortbread, but returned from time to time as tangerine creams, although with a fresh acidity which might be tangerine peel. The taste is crisp, acidic and lightly sweet, and the finish warming. Water raises Acid Drops (boiled sweets), and more mandarin oranges (fresh this time), with a background note of rice pudding. The texture is soft; the taste fresh and acidic overall. An attractive aperitif malt.

Next, a slightly more technical appraisal of a sample of Glengoyne, at the same age, but this time drawn from a single ex-sherry cask:

GLENGOYNE 1997
12YO Highland @57.2%Vol
(Cask No: 582)

Appearance: Polished mahogany. From a first fill, European oak ex-sherry butt. Good beading. Good legs.

Aroma: No nose prickle, in spite of its strength. Immediate scents of crème brûlée (or creamy custard with burnt sugar), backed by fresh Virginian pipe tobacco and behind this a faint whiff of treacle toffee. As might be expected, a little water raises a brimstone note, but at an acceptable level (and it blows off after a while); then caramel coated in dark chocolate, with dried fruits (especially figs).

Taste: The aromas noted at full strength translate well into tastes. Tannic and slightly bitter overall, as in bitter chocolate. A lingering aftertaste of sherry and dark chocolate. Becomes softer and more oily at reduced strength; a rich, fruity sweetness followed by a tannic dryness. Medium length, with a dark chocolate and Madeira aftertaste.

Comment: The flavour profile is typical of maturation in a good European oak, ex-sherry butt. After 12 years in this active vessel, there is not much evidence of the original spirit character, but the cask has done an excellent job – and the whisky has been bottled at just the right time, before the wood takes over.

Here are a couple of notes I wrote recently for the World of Whiskies Duty Free Shops, to appear on their website and in their airport shops.

THE DALMORE CIGAR MALT RESERVE
Single Highland Malt Whisky @ 44%Vol

Tasting Note: Deep amber, with copper lights. Brightly polished mahogany glittering in the light of an open fire... Maybe my imagination, but the first impression is of straight Virginia tobacco (Gold Flake perhaps), with hard toffee and dry fruit cake (topped with toasted almonds and glacé cherries), also dried figs (more precisely 'Fig Pigs', for those who remember them!). Tasted straight, the texture is smooth and mouthfilling; the taste sweeter than the nose suggests, but with a zestiness and robustness, and a warming spicy/gingery finish, with lingering dark chocolate in the aftertaste.

With a drop of water, the aroma moves to fruit cake mix to start, then more toffee emerges – perhaps banoffee pie – with a trace of orange peel. The texture is now even smoother, but still pleasantly spicy as you swallow. A relatively short finish, but a delicious warming sensation.

Occasion: Perfectly compliments a robust cigar, dark chocolate and black coffee.

Comment: A comfortable dram. Easy drinking. Enjoyable with or without a cigar, especially after a meal.

GLENMORANGIE ARTEIN
Single Highland Malt @ 46%Vol
Sassicaia Finished

A striking peach colour, with slow, viscous legs – indicating good texture. The initial scent is mineralic and matches the whisky's name ('stone' in Gaelic). Immediately behind this are fruity notes

– peach predominating. Sweet, soft and comforting. As it warms in the hand it becomes distinctly peppery/spicy on the nose, and this is reflected by the taste: a spicy fizz across the tongue. A voluptuous texture, with a sweet start and a dry finish leaving an aftertaste of peaches (again!).

Drinks well straight, but a dash of water opens up the aroma – now reminiscent of the interior of a new Aston Martin, with heady floral notes. A smooth mouthfeel and a sweet taste, enlivened by traces of lemon sherbet sweets (also detectable in the aroma after a while), with continuing pepperiness and later a distinct taste of Nuttella chocolate and hazelnut spread. A lengthy, nutty warming finish.

Occasion: Instead of champagne at Ascot.

Comment: An outstanding addition to Glenmorangie's distinguished range.

John Glaser, the talented and innovative master blender at Compass Box, asked me to comment on his blended malt (i.e. is mix of malts from various distilleries), Spice Tree:

THE SPICE TREE
'Double-matured' Blended Malt from Compass Box @ 46%Vol

Initial fruity aromas (especially above the rim of the glass) of dried apricots and brambles, with a curious bosky background. Difficult to pin down – almost smoky, but not quite; perhaps a hint of rapeseed oil. Changing continually: now an artificial strawberry scent and a whiff of Young's 303 gun oil. Perhaps vanilla ice-cream drizzled with strawberry.

Water reduces the nose considerably and makes it more 'ordinary' and familiar.

The taste, at full strength, is sweet and hot. At about 30% it has a smooth mouthfeel and an excellent balance – some sweetness and light acidity, drying gently in the finish; still warming. The 'spice' comes right at the end and in the aftertaste – more allspice or nutmeg than pepper (although there is a hint of the latter, white pepper, in the aftertaste).

I poured myself another glass immediately! A charming autumnal whisky – 'mists and mellow fruitfulness'.

There is no need to be analytical and pseudo-scientific in your approach to writing a tasting note. Here is a narrative inspired by a young Islay malt identified merely as 'Sample 24', written for The Scotch Malt Whisky Society some years ago and used (in its entirety!) on the bottle's label.

SAMPLE 24 THROUGH THE LOOKING GLASS

We enter a white room, a tabula rasa – perhaps John Updike's white sheet of paper, 'radiant as the sun rising in the morning', or Kandinski's freshly sized canvass, 'pregnant with all possibility'.

We find it unnerving, but not unduly ominous. We have been in similar rooms before. There is a profound silence here; the temperature is neither hot nor cold; the atmosphere, at least to begin with, is not oppressive, even when the door by which we have entered merges with the white wall. There are no windows, and although the room is bright, no immediately discernable source of light. An operating theatre comes to mind, and this sets going a butterfly-tremble in our guts.

Inevitably, our attention is focussed upon the glass which stands alone on a white table in the middle of the room. Mercifully, bearing no similarity to an operating table. It is a tulip glass, a bulbous copita, and contains what looks like vin gris – a pale liquid, the colour of tarnished silver shot with lime, glittering in the even light. Beside it is a flask of water.

We take up the glass and sniff. The physical sensation is both peppery and nettley. Then the visions begin…

The room is now a kitchen. On a formica dresser is an Arbroath smokie, half unwrapped from its waxed paper packet. A pan of gooseberries is bubbling on the stove. The sink is full of dirty dishes and very soapy hot water, and the scent from this mingles with a background of artificial air-freshener.

A large, raw-boned, somewhat ill-kempt woman in her thirties is cleaning a window with a cloth soaked in spirituous cleaning fluid which smells of vinyl and antiseptic. The cloth squeaks across the glass…

To clear the mirror, as it were, we take a sip from the copita. The flavour is very hot – at once fiery and spicy and etheric – Fisherman's Friend lozenges. Aggressively acidic and salty, with distant diesel fumes. We hastily add water.

Now we are observing a fishing boat, moored alongside a pier. The boat's diesel engine is running and puffing grey smoke. In a moment, we notice it is not only the engine that is making smoke: the woman we encountered earlier is now reducing seal blubber in a pot over a brazier, which she is stoking with bits of tyre and animal bones. She is wearing a Burberry baseball cap and a PVC apron. Fishing nets lie on the deck, with the dry remains of prawns and crabs entangled in them. Bladder-wrack clings to the pier, whispering.

Seaweed imbues the flavour of the liquid – iodine and operating theatres; a taste which begins sweet, becomes acidic and salty; a texture at once oily and spritzich, as if the seaweed had been sprinkled with cayenne pepper. Smouldering tractor tyres still linger in the mouth, and our final vision is of a friendly, Burberry crowned, face saying:

'Whit yoos want?'

Here is an entirely different approach, where the 'analysis' is turned into a story, inspired by the scents and tastes of the whisky. Balblair Distillery is where the auction takes place in the film.

BALBLAIR 2001
Single Highland Malt @46%Vol

The aunt poured half a teacup of pale gold liquid - bright but slightly dull - into a dainty porcelain receptacle, not much bigger than an egg cup.

'China?', says I.

'Dear boy, you know I never drink tea in the afternoon. I follow Mr Churchill's example...'

This allusion was lost on me. She pushed the cake stand within reach and having missed lunch, I commandeered a brace of cucumber sandwiches (dainty; brown bread and butter) and a slice of Battenburg which, it has to be said, looked as if it had appeared before on the tea-table: the marzipan was curling a bit and the pale pink sponge looked dry, but I can never resist old Batters...

Only then did I have a sip of 'tea'.

'I say...', I spluttered. 'What have we here?'

She said nothing, smiled mysteriously and observed me quizzically through her lorgnette.

I addressed the cup again and sniffed it. At that moment a waft of salty sea air floated through the window from the beach and seemed to bring with it the scent of ice cream cornets. Or was this scent coming from the liquid?

The taste was sweet, then slightly salty, with a green apple element.

'Top hole!', says I. 'What on earth is it?'

Now I was smelling Parma violets - but surely this was the aunt - and a scent of Makassar spirit, as in barbers' shops, as she refilled my cup.

'Scotch malt whisky from a distillery called Balblair in the far north of Scotland. Do you approve?'

'Rather! Must tell Jeeves to get me some.'

Film Credits

Poster for the French release. © Tomi Ungerer.

Sixteen Films
Why Not Productions
Wild Bunch

BFI
Les Films du Fleuve
Urania Pictures
France 2 Cinéma

Canal+
Cinécinéma
Soficinéma
Le Pacte
Cinéart
France Télévisions
Canto Bros Productions

Director	Ken Loach
Producer	Rebecca O'Brien
Screenplay	Paul Laverty
Executive Producers	Pascal Caucheteux
	Vincent Maraval
Music	George Fenton
Editor	Jonathan Morris
Line Producer	Peter Gallagher
Sound Editor	Kevin Brazier
Locations	Michael Higson
Assistant Directors	David Gilchrist
	Michael Queen
Costume Designer	Carole K Fraser
Casting	Kahleen Crawford
Recordist	Ray Beckett
Photography	Robbie Ryan
Production Designer	Fergus Clegg
Robbie	Paul Brannigan
Leonie	Siobhan Reilly

Harry	John Henshaw
Albert	Gary Maitland
Rhino	William Ruane
Mo	Jasmin Riggins
Willy	Scott Dymond
Clancy	Scott Kyle
Sniper	Neil Leiper
Dougie	James Casey
Caz	Caz Dunlop
Matt	Gilbert Martin
Sheriff	Stewart Preston
Procurator Fiscal	Vincent Friell
Defence Lawyers	Kirstin Murray
	Nick Farr
	Charles Jamieson
Station Master	Ford Kiernan
Thaddeus	Roger Allam
Rory McAllister	Charles MacLean
Dobie	David Goodall
Auctioneer	Bruce Addison
North American	Paul Birchard
Volunteer Tasters	Jimmy Chisholm
	John P. Arnold
Mairi	Joy McAvoy
Anthony	Roderick Cowie
Anthony's Family	Alison McGinnes
	Andy McLaren
	Kelly Scott
Anthony's Girlfriend	Lynsey Lawrie
Moderator	Robert McHarg
Grace	Lynsey-Anne Moffatt
Policemen	Jim Sweeney
	Russell Anderson
Baby Luke	Zac Reilly

And

Elizabeth Porter, Ted Davitt, Lorne MacFadyen, Eric Robertson, Charlene Keating, James Ramsay, Pauline Glynn, Lee Fanning, Daniel Portman, Charlie Miller, Paul Donnelly, Barrie Hunter, Dai Tabuchi, Kasumi Katano, Chooye Bay, Siu Hun Li, Lorene Bonino, Caroline Franco, Susana Tejero Fernández, Puri Salgado

Production	Eimhear McMahon
	Steven Moore
	Fergus Cook
	Jack Thomas-O'Brien
3rd Assistant Director	Stephen Carney
Floor Runner	Marilyn Edmond
Floor Runner/Unit Medic	Alex McKay
Casting Assistant	Caroline Stewart
Unit Manager	Robbie Kirkpatrick
Locations Assistants	Chris Cameron
	Gerry MacLeod
Drivers	Jas Brown
	Happy Harrop
Focus Puller	John Watters
Clapper loaders	Amaury Duquenne
	Joachim Philippe
	Leo Lefevre
Camera Trainee	Iftekhar Gafar
2nd Camera	Alastair Rae
	Barry Ackroyd
2nd Camera Focus Puller	Anna Benbow
	Olly Driscoll
2nd Camera Clapper Loaders	Grant McPhee
	Glenn Coulman
	Ian Jackson
Boom Operator	Pete Murphy
Sound Assistant	Neal Skillen
Gaffer	Andy Cole
Electricians	Antoine Doyen
	Laurent Van Eijs
Dailies	Stuart Farmer
	John Hutton
	Niall Smith
	David Mitchell
Art Director	Zoe Wight
Standby Art Director	Rhian Nicholas
Stand-in Art Director	Susan Collin
Prop Buyer	Craig Menzies

Prop Master	Tony Sheridan
Dressing Props	Fred MacMillan
	Paul Lambie
Standby Props	Campbell Mitchell
Petty Cash Buyer	Aoife McKim
Action vehicles Co-ordinator	Ronnie Morrison
Props Dailies	Liam McCallum
	Dave MacLeod
	Andrew Neilson
Construction Manager	Danny Sumsion
Carpenters	Alex Robertson
	David Richmond
Painters	Paul Curren
	Bobby Gee
Stagehands	Jason Strachan
	Jake Drummond
Riggers	Billy Wilson
	Ross Pearson
Construction Dailies	Sam Curren
	Bobby Hughes
	Phil Bowen
Make-up Designer	Karen Brotherston
Costumer Supervisor	Dani Millar
Make-up Assistant	Claire Harris
Armourers	Jim Elliott
	Mark Reilly
Stunt Co-ordinator	Paul Heasman
Script Consultant	Roger Smith
Script Supervisor	Susanna Lenton
Stills Photographer	Joss Barratt
Production Accountant	Tina Shadick
Assistant Production Accountant	Habib Rahman
Auditor	Malde & Co.
1st Assistant Editor	Paul Clegg
Effects Editor/Foley Recordist	Robert Brazier
Dialogue/Foley Editor	Ben Brazier

Foley Artist	Rowena Wilkinson
	Sue Harding
Sound Transfer	Steve Carr
Re-recording Mixers	Ian Tapp CAS
	Andrew Caller
Caterers	BC TV & Film Caterers
Security	Media Security Scotland
Music recorded by	Steve Price
	Angel Recording Studio
Pro Tools	Jeremy Murphy
Music Co-ordinator	Nicole Jacob
Drums	Ian Thomas
Bass	Steve Pearce
Guitars	Steve Donnelly
	John Parricelli
Percussion	Frank Ricotti

'Some Chords' performed by Deadmau5
Licensed courtesy of Virgin Records Limited
Written by Joel Zimmerman
Published by EMI Music Publishing Limited

'I'm Gonna Be (500 Miles)' performed by The Proclaimers
Licensed courtesy of EMI Records Ltd.
Written by Charles Stobo Reid / Craig Morris Reid
©1988 Zoo Music Ltd. All rights administered
by Warner/Chappell Music Ltd.

With thanks to:
Kenny MacAskill, Angus McConnell, Andy Laverty, John Carnochan &
Glasgow Violence Reduction Unit; and to all who shared their
experiences with us while doing Community Payback.

Charlie McLean, Andrew Bell, Frank McHardy, Sukhinder Singh, Jane
Martin & Staff, Lillian Cringles & Staff, Graham Lamb, Bobby Campbell,
Linda Nimmo, Raymond McQuillan & Staff, George Smith, Dennis
Docherty, Staff and Young People of Polmont Youth Offenders Institution,
Chrissy McGeever, Keith McLauchlin, Professor Andrew Coyle,

Bill McKinlay, Laura Coltart, John May, Johnny Bradford & 'Moving On'
Trust, Paul Gilhooley, Bobby Stewart, Paul Kelly, Govanhill Youth Project,
Kirsty Laverty, Ben Adams, Sacro.

Scottish Railway Preservation Society, Glasgow Sheriff Court,
Tron St Mary's, Red Road; Queen Mother's Hospital, Queen's Cross
Housing Association, Caledonian Hilton Hotel, Edinburgh Film Focus,
Edinburgh City Council, The Saracen Head, Glasgow City Council,
Strathclyde Police, Amar Aslam, Sandra McLaren, Danny Jackson; and the
colleges, schools, youth groups and community centres of Glasgow
who donated their time.

Inver House Distilleries, Burn Stewart & Ian MacLeod,
and the staff of Balblair, Deanston and Glengoyne distilleries

Ben Nevis, Berry Brothers & Rudd, Bladnoch Distillery, Bruichladdich
Distillery, Dewar & Sons, Edrington Group, Glenmorangie Distillers,
Gordon & MacPhail, Isle of Arran Distillery, J&G Grant,
Laphroaig Distillery, Loch Lomond Distillers, Morrison Bowmore,
Springbank Distillers, Tu libardine, Whyte & Mackay,
William Grant & Sons

Lawyer	Stephen Grosz
	Bindmans LLP
Insurance	Media Insurance Brokers
For Why Not Productions	Grigie Soryar
	Etienne de Ricaud
	Lucie Borleteau
For Les Films du Fleuve	Delphine Tomson
	Tania Antonioli
	Marie-Antoinette
	Schoenmaeckers
For Wild Bunch	Marie Besançon
	Emmanuelle Castro
For BFI	Tanya Seghatchian
	Natascha Wharton
	Will Evans
	Ian Kirk
	Fiona Morham

Financing
With the support of the Tax Shelter of the Belgian Federal Government
Inver Invest, Olivier Bronckart, Jacques-Henri Bronckart, Garage P. Schyns
Liège, GHL Groupe, André Lemaire, Urban Invest, Courtier d'assurance
Losange Dhondt, Cash Converters, BAO Assurances de l'Ourthe, Avise
Glasgow Film Office, Creative Scotland.

Titles Design	Martin Butterworth
	Creative Partnership
Laboratory	Clive Noakes
	Deluxe Laboratories
Neg Cutter	Steve Farman
Film Stock	Kodak Belgium
Camera and Lighting Equipment	Eye Lite Group
Cutting Room	Goldcrest Post
Digital Post Production	Len Brown, Molinare
Sound Re-recording	Pinewood Studios
International Sales	Wild Bunch

Filmed on location in Scotland

The characters and incidents portrayed and the names used herein are
fictitious, and any similarity to any name or incident, or the character or
biography of any person, is purely coincidental and unintentional

Made through the British Film Institute's Film Fund

Awarding funds through The National Lottery

A British / French / Belgian / Italian Co-Production

© Sixteen Films Ltd, Why Not Productions S.A., Wild Bunch S.A.,
Urania Pictures, Les Films du Fleuve, France 2 Cinéma,
British Film Institute
MMXII

Route Irish
Written by Paul Laverty, Directed by Ken Loach
ISBN: 978-1901927-47-4

In September 2004, Fergus persuaded his best mate Frankie to join his security team in Baghdad: Together they risked their lives in a city steeped in violence, terror and greed, and awash with billions of US dollars. Three years later, Frankie is killed on Route Irish, the most dangerous road in the world. Back in Liverpool, a grief-stricken Fergus rejects the official explanation that Frankie was simply in the wrong place at the wrong time, and begins his own investigation into his soul mate's death.

Features the full screenplay, character backstory, production notes and photographs from the film, plus background essays by Mark Townsend, Haifa Zangana and Mike Phipps.

Even the Rain
Written by Paul Laverty, Directed by Icíar Bollaín
ISBN: 978-1907862-05-2

Costa and Sebastian arrive in Cochabamba, Bolivia, to shoot a period film about Columbus's arrival in the Americas. Sebastian wants to upturn the entire conservative myth of Western Civilisation's arrival in the Americas as a force for good. The battle to get their film made intertwines with the fight of their Bolivian crew members, deprived of their most basic rights, prohibited from collecting even the rain.

Looking For Eric
Written by Paul Laverty, Directed by Ken Loach
ISBN: 978-1901927-41-2

Eric the postman is slipping through his own fingers... Can he face Lily, the woman he once loved thirty years ago? Despite outrageous efforts and misplaced goodwill from his football fan mates, Eric continues to sink. In desperate times it takes a spliff and a special friend from foreign parts to challenge a lost postman to make that journey into the most perilous territory of all – the past. As the Chinese, and one Frenchman, say, 'He who is afraid to throw the dice, will never throw a six.'

For further information on these books,
and other titles from Route please visit:

www.route-online.com